Häagen-Dazs is

its own reward

Celebrating virtue ethics

Ellyn Ritterskamp

i

Printed in the United States of America

First Printing, 2015. Second Edition, 2015.

ISBN 0692355596

ISBN-13 978-0692355596

Contact: elritter@uncc.edu

Ellyn Ritterskamp earned a B.A. in Philosophy and two Master's degrees from UNC Charlotte, and has taught ethics and philosophy there since 2003. She also has worked at The Charlotte Observer and in the McClatchy Publishing Center since 1988. She has appeared on three TV game shows, and has visited all the Major League Baseball parks, all the South Atlantic League parks, and all of the Carolina League parks.

Introduction

Do you know a person of virtue? Do you know someone who always seems to do the right thing and resists all temptations?

What does it mean to you to be virtuous? Does it mean behaving correctly, according to a social or religious standard? Sometimes virtue has come to be associated only with abstinence, chastity and refraining from particular behaviors. This use of the word has cost us much of its larger meaning.

Virtue is about excellence and being the best people we can be. It is not an attempt to prescribe our every movement or word. Aristotle said that as we perform virtuous acts, we become virtuous people. It's not certain that good acts lead to the correct state of soul, because sometimes we just do things out of rote and not for the right reasons. If we abstain from an action only so we won't get caught doing it, we are not behaving out of virtue but out of self-interest. But if we abstain because that choice arises naturally from the character we have constructed for ourselves, we can call that virtue.

I'll explain all of this in more detail later. For now, the key is that we all can be people of virtue. It is within our reach. It is a lifelong pursuit, but it does not have to be a struggle. If you believe you have not been a virtuous person, you can change, even though you may be afraid. If you believe you are partway on the road to a virtuous state of soul, this book may help you travel even further. If you feel that you are already completely virtuous, you are only reading these pages to see if my take on it is the same as yours -- but no one is completely virtuous. Everybody has something to work on.

Dedication

I am grateful to my parents, Julie and Jack H. Ritterskamp Jr., for encouraging my brothers and me to be responsible citizens and to use our talents to make the world better. And to read.

I am grateful to Dr. Samuel D. Watson, Jr., for many encouraging moments and also for writing on one of my early college papers: "Dear Ellyn, You have a delightful felicity with words. Try not to let that stand in the way of your actually having something to say."

Ever since then, I have tried to have something worth saying, or keep quiet.

Credits

Editor: Reid Creager

Illustrations: Brian Cetina

Photo: Dan Avila

Note: The second edition has a new cover, a new typeface, and slightly less technical language throughout the first three chapters.

CHAPTER 1

Some Ethics Explained

Why would we choose a virtue-based way of life? The other ways are easier, because they have rules. You follow the rule, and everything is all right. But if you construct a virtuous character, there are no rules. It is harder.

I'll tell you about some of the rules-based ways first.

In the history of philosophy, virtue arrived pretty early, with the ancient Greeks. The thinker whose ideas I'll draw on most was Aristotle, who lived from 384-322 BCE. He studied with Plato, who learned from Socrates. Aristotle liked to define things, down to the last bit. He was interested in understanding the essence of a thing; he said that the excellence of a thing comes from how well it fulfills its purpose.

For Aristotle, excellence and virtue are the same notion. Horses should run, stand so many inches tall, and eat grass. If a horse does these things well, it fulfills its nature and is a good or excellent horse. Trees should grow, perhaps they should provide shade, and perhaps they should provide fruit. If they do these things, they are good trees or excellent trees. What is it about human beings that can make them excellent? It is our ability to reason and to choose what kind of people we want to be. Because we can choose, we should choose to be good. Otherwise we are not excellent -- we are only existing.

At first, being good requires tremendous effort. Our inclination is to take the easy path, to be lazy or selfish. We rise above that inclination, though, and choose to work hard and be generous to others. If we stayed selfish and lazy, we would be like a bad horse or a bad tree, and not fulfill our potential. We have the capacity for greatness, if we are willing to work at it. The trick is convincing ourselves to be willing to work at it.

After the Greeks came the early Christians, who began meeting all sorts of cultures and ethical systems as they spread. They had some especially interesting interactions with African and Muslim thinkers. It's always good to talk to other people about your ideas. The ideas get stronger if they are good, and they get amended if the other people have something else to say that seems to fit your idea. If nothing else, this interaction with Islam eased the transition from a system with many gods to a system with just one god. Long after the Greeks came two ethical systems we still use today, developed about 200 years ago: utilitarianism and deontology.

Utilitarianism

The idea of utilitarianism, or utility ethics, is to figure out which action will bring the greatest happiness to the greatest number of people. Sounds nice, doesn't it? But different things and different ideas make different people happy. Some people want comfortable families; some want material wealth; some want health. It is probably true that most of us want most of the same things, but maybe in different quantities.

Jeremy Bentham and John Stuart Mill developed utility ethics. Bentham, in particular, thought that if we asked every person what made her happy, we could have a chart that listed it all. The chart would even assign points to the things that the most people wanted. That way, if we were trying to choose between one action or another, we could look at the chart to see how many points were attached to each result. Then it would be easy to know what to do.

You see why this wouldn't work. Sometimes people are not wise enough to know that a thing that will make them happy now will make them unhappy later. So we need a way to show people that sometimes a long-term happiness is better than a short-term happiness. Some other ancient Greeks besides Aristotle, the Stoics and the Epicureans, were on the right track toward explaining this notion about the short term and the long term. They understood that eating and drinking too much made them sick later, so they tried to live in moderation in order to live longer and be healthier. A long time later, the utility ethics people grasped the same thing.

Mill said that when we face a dilemma, the principle of utility helps us decide how many people will benefit by our action. This helps us decide which action to take. He thought that morality should concern others because we are social creatures who desire communion with others. As such, we must consider the well-being of others along with our own well-being. It is appropriate that we come to align our feelings with the success of our society. "The good of others becomes ... a thing naturally and necessarily to be attended to." (33)

Utility ethicists came to see that a thing that is good for one person might be very bad for the rest of the group. They understood the need for a system that helps us figure out what is best for the most people in the group.

For example, slavery in the American South was good for the plantation owners because it allowed them to farm their land efficiently. It was bad for the slaves and the families they left behind. Plantation owners did not understand that slavery was bad for them in the long run. It was bad for them because it made them think it was acceptable to treat other human beings like a lower species. It was bad for them because they were perpetuating a wrongness on humanity, a wrongness that still exists today in some places.

Utility ethics would ask us to consider the well-being and happiness of all members of a society, not just the ones in its upper caste. The word "utility" has to do with use and usefulness. When we think about human moral progress, we see that it was not useful for us to be sidetracked when we believed that subjugating other humans was aceptable. It was not useful because it held us back from true moral progress.

We can consider other examples to show how utility ethics would help deal with a problem. Peter Singer, a contemporary utilitarian, is an advocate of improving the treatment of animals. He believes in humans learning to treat other species well.

He also has some ideas about how to put a value on human life -- ideas that some consider radical. He believes we spend too much effort and money keeping sick people alive, when maybe they and we would be better off if we let them go. He believes the rare babies who are born without brains should be put to death early, rather than letting them live only the few weeks they can survive. He believes this is merciful, and that the money spent keeping them alive could be better spent on someone who has hope of living.

This is not easy stuff. Utility ethics is about what is best for all of us, not just what is best for an individual.

They tackled utility ethics in *Star Trek* many times. Creator Gene Roddenberry was a big philosophy fan; any idea worth contemplating ended up in one of his scripts somewhere. This issue of what is best for the most people arose in the second and third Star Trek feature movies. At the end of the second movie, *The Wrath of Khan*, Science Officer Spock has voluntarily entered an engine chamber to stop a process that would destroy the ship. The chamber has been flooded with radiation; he knows he will die. He is able to speak to his friends through the transparent shielding. As they realize he must die, one of them asks him why he gave himself up. "Because the needs of the many outweigh the needs of the few," he says.

It was very sad, and we thought he was lost forever. But they revived him in the next movie, *The Search for Spock*, and he asked why. "The needs of the one outweighed the needs of the many," his best friend said. I struggled with this for a while but then decided that a universe with Spock was better than a universe without him. In that fictional universe, Spock later did so much good for humanity and other races that any sacrifice his friends made to revive him was easily repaid.

Utility ethics is a nice way to think about ourselves in the context of a larger society. We can ask ourselves if the action we are about to take will benefit many folks, and if it is a short-term benefit or long-term benefit. Sometimes I vote for a candidate who does not represent my views because I believe this candidate will be better for the society over the next few years than the one who is more like me. Utility is about being useful, and usefulness is a concept worth contemplating.

Deontology

Around the same time as utilitarianism came a system called deontology, or duty ethics, developed by German thinker Immanuel Kant. It says all that matters is that we take the right action, regardless of the consequence. He said we must act not only to conform with moral law but for the sake of it. He said we must build ethical law on reason alone, that we must act in such a way that we would have the principle behind our action be a universal maxim -- that the rule would apply to everyone in the same situation. We cannot make exceptions for ourselves; doing so would mean he law is not universal.

His conditions for morality are that we have a good will and that we be rational beings. He said that a simple desire to make others happy (like the utilitarians) is not enough to constitute morality; a moral act must come from duty. Only duty. This is his first principle of morality.

His second principle is that an action attains moral worth only from its having followed moral law. Moral worth is not measured by results or consequences, only by motivation.

Kant believed in an absolute right and that we find it by universalizing our actions. What that means is, if I want to take an action, I ask myself, "How would it be if everyone in this same situation took this exact same action?" If I am willing to live in that world, my action is probably right. If I think that would be a bad place, my action is probably wrong. When I approach an intersection with a traffic light, I must stop if the light is red. If it is yellow, I must get all the way through the intersection by the time it turns red. If I do not stop when I am expected to stop, someone else will come from the cross-street, and we will have a collision. As I do not want there to be collisions at intersections, I observe the traffic signals. I do not observe them because I don't want to get a ticket; I observe them because to do so makes things safer for all drivers. This action is a right action, because I have appealed to its universality and found it good.

One of the classic examples of deciding whether an act is right or wrong is a scenario in which you're in the house with your brother. A man with a gun comes to the front door and asks you where your brother is. You know where your brother is, but you also know the man will kill your brother if you tell him. Some ethical systems will allow you to lie to the man with the gun because you are saving your brother's life. Duty ethics, however, says that lying is always wrong. There are no exceptions. You must tell the man with the gun where your brother is. It may turn out that he kills your brother. It may turn out he is there to protect your brother from someone else. For Kant, the consequence does not matter. It is important to him that we follow the universal law, that we do not begin to make exceptions for ourselves. He believes we do not want to live in a world where there is any instance in which lying is appropriate. If we do, we never know when someone is lying. We must have concrete, absolute reliability, or everything goes to pieces.

Duty ethics makes things easy, in the sense that once you know the rules, all you have to do is follow them. You don't have to make any choices. Now and then a crisis may arise that is not in your rule book, but all you have to do to solve it is figure out which universal law is attached to it. This system is very helpful sometimes, because we do run into situations that are not covered in our experience. We don't have rules for every problem, so sometimes it's handy to ask, "How would the world be if everyone in this situation took this exact action?" The tricky part is, sometimes we cannot anticipate the answer to that question. We have to just do something and hope it is right, then find out later what the result was. Maybe then we can predict what the world would look like if lots of people took the same action.

It might just be that there's a way we can know we will take the right action, even if we can't always calculate the happiness of society or the universality of the law. I believe there's a system that sets us up for success -- not so much with laws and charts but with habits. This system is the first one we discussed. Virtue.

I'll explain more about what virtue really is in Chapter 2. In Chapter 3 we will look at a specific ethical problem from several angles. In Chapter 4 I'll describe four modern virtues, the ones I think are most important. In Chapter 5 we will take on the hard part, which is changing ourselves. Chapter 6 is about why we should make the attempt to be good. By then I hope you will see what is so fulfilling and productive about a life of virtue and that it does not have to be hard. I am excited you have come this far.

You must already have the virtues of fortitude and determination!

CHAPTER 2

The Golden Mean

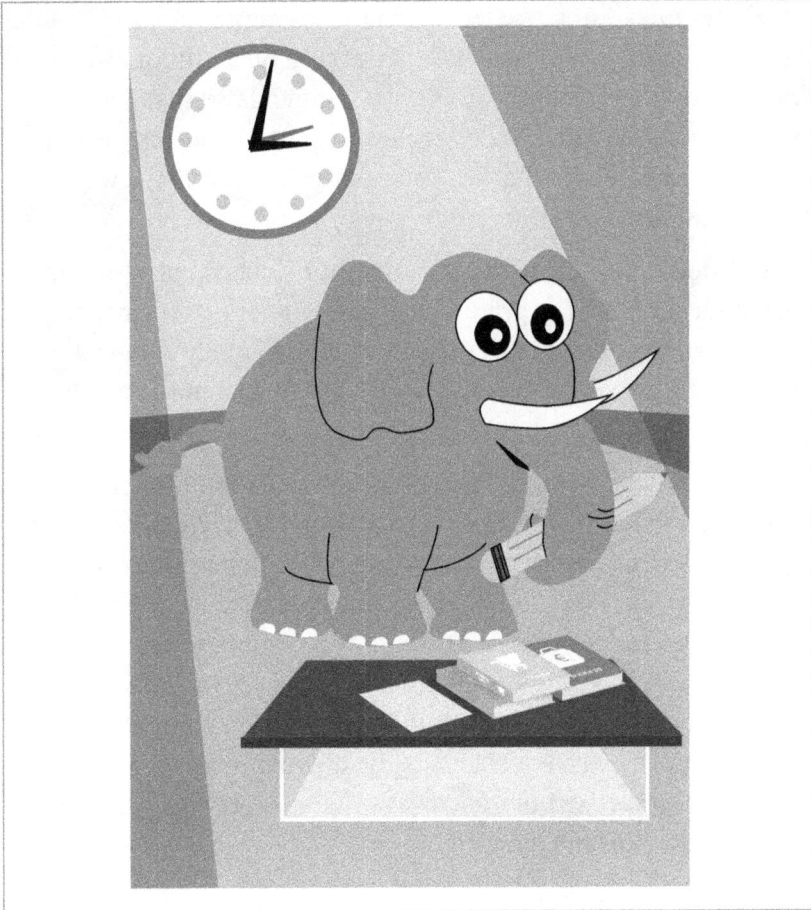

For $100: According to an old saying, what quality "is its own reward"?

A. melancholy B. virtue

C. humor D. Häagen-Dazs

The answer is virtue, of course. Virtue is its own reward. I was asked that question a few years ago in a remarkable setting (a television quiz show called "Who Wants to Be a Millionaire"). The answer came easily, but I realized much later that I had never considered what the statement meant. It was just one of those quotable things that we hear all the time and rarely contemplate.

I decided to contemplate it. I thought a doctoral program in philosophy at a nearby graduate school would be the place for me to learn enough about virtue to be able to analyze the sentence "Virtue is its own reward." That turned out not to be necessary.

In high school, I wanted to attend a particular university but couldn't afford it. I later found out we can learn wherever we are. It doesn't have to be a particular, prestigious place. I've found the same thing about studying virtue. It's not where we are that matters but what we do. I may have intuitively known what virtue is, but now I think I've learned how to explain it -- not so much by reading and studying it as by teaching it. That's the best way to learn some things: by having to repackage them for someone else. Virtue was always there; I just never had ways to explain it. Now maybe I do.

Is virtue its own reward? The short answer is, "Yes."

To get to the longer answer, we have to examine the ideas of virtue and of reward. Virtue is not so much about having particular measurable good qualities of character which would earn rewards; instead, think of it as a broader state of soul.

So what is virtue theory? I explained in Chapter 1 about utility ethics and duty ethics, and why I think virtue has more possibilities. The way Plato and Aristotle talked about it a long time ago, and the way the professional philosophers talk about it now, is called virtue theory. The neat part is that we are going to put it into practice -- because with stuff like this, there's not much point in working out a theory or a system, if you don't then put it into action.

We will begin with early discussions of virtue.

Plato's vision of virtue is that we cultivate a state of soul in which we dwell in goodness. Living within this good state, we are not so concerned with performing moral actions. For Plato, we experience an ongoing willingness to be good. The virtues take care of themselves.

One of the Greek words we use to think about virtue is *arête*, which has to do with excellence. We are striving for excellent characters. For Aristotle, discovering an appropriate middle path between a defect and an excess of a character trait is how we exhibit excellence. He acknowledges that finding these paths is an ongoing process, as they fluctuate with the situation. This does not mean that our morality is relative in a bad way. It means that each character trait is on a spectrum, and our particular traits should fall somewhere near the middle of that spectrum. He calls it the Golden Mean.

Think back to math class and finding an average. That's what the mean is. For example, you have five items valued 1, 4, 5, 7, and 10, you add them up (27) and divide by the numbers of items, and you get 5.4. That's the average, and the arithmetic mean. If you had 10 equally spaced items from 1-10, the mean would be right in the middle, at 5.5 (the mathematics term is median). But Aristotle understood that we are not perfect, and that sometimes it is appropriate not to be exactly in the middle. The right place to be on that sliding scale is what he called the Golden Mean.

He discussed many different virtues, separating them into moral virtues and intellectual virtues. He said that the mean is the middle path, between the excess of a trait on one side, and its defect on the other. So he was saying you do not want to have too much of a quality, nor too little. A good example of a trait that shows this is courage. We want to have courage in the proper amount. You can see that having too little courage would be cowardice. But what would be the result of having too much courage? You could become reckless or foolhardy, and dash into danger without any thought for safety. This disregard for danger is not courage. Courage is bravery in the face of fear, not the absence of fear. Perhaps after some experience, you can be said to be courageous even if you are not afraid, but certainly not at first. We must learn to push on in spite of our fears, and then we eventually learn to brush them aside or not to feel them at all. We'll talk more about courage in the next chapter.

Aristotle also explained what he thought was a good middle path of the virtue of generosity, which means giving to others out of the proper motivation. He called it liberality, but that word has come to be associated with political views, so we will use the word generosity instead. The excess of this virtue would be someone who gives money, hoping for accolades from others who will praise him for his generosity. There is an appropriate amount of praise for such gifts, and the giver should not wish for more -- if he does, then the gift has become centered on the person and not on the good that the money can do. This is not real generosity but vanity. We will also address generosity in the next chapter, as it is a very important virtue.

The deficiency of generosity is seen in the person who has money to spare but does not spare it. The person who will not do this out of greed or selfishness lacks the virtue of generosity.

Pride is our next virtue. I did not realize until recently that pride is not a vice but a virtue. It must be handled correctly, because it is very easy to slip into an excess of pride that becomes vanity. Pride is an appropriate appreciation of our own goodness. If it becomes inappropriate because we think we are very good but we really are not then it becomes egoism. This is one of the deficiencies of pride (the other being a kind of low self-esteem). The excess of pride is vanity, in which we are very concerned with having other people appreciate our goodness.

The golden mean is the place in the middle where we understand that we are good, that we are still becoming good, and we can appreciate that state and effort. That's it. There is no meaning attached to the opinion of other people. When we become concerned with what other people think of us, we have left the middle of the spectrum and are headed toward one of the ends. That is not a place of virtue.

The last virtue we'll look at in this chapter is anger. You may be thinking, "why is anger a virtue?" I felt the same way until Aristotle made me see that sometimes it is correct to feel anger. At its excess, anger is dangerous and uncomfortable. We have all seen its effects when people get too angry and allow their tempers to explode. They inevitably harm themselves or someone else. This kind of anger is unhealthy, whether it is directed at one's self or at another.

You might think this would end our conversation about anger, because you would think there could not be a deficiency of it. In the other virtues, we have seen a clear excess and a deficiency. Anger also has a deficiency. There are times when we should be morally outraged, when we see that an injustice is being done. There are times when we should see that a person or plant or animal is being mistreated, and we should be angry. We should be angry enough to take action, to point out the problem, or to try to solve it. Just like with other virtues, there is a place in the middle where we want to land. With anger, most of the time we want it to be dormant. Only rarely do we need to summon some passion and outrage. When it's time, we want to be committed about it.

Aristotle talked about lots of other virtues, which we will look at briefly. If you want to read more about this, the book is called *The Nichomachean Ethics*. It's named for his son, who edited it. Some of the other moral virtues he addressed are justice, temperance, friendliness, truthfulness and shame (which he says is a quasi-virtue but nonetheless interesting).

Justice is the sense of right we feel when fairness is done, when people are getting what they deserve. We can think of it as being about restoring balance.

Temperance is the ability to hold a middle path and not be too extreme in our behaviors. We can also call this virtue moderation.

Aristotle's discussion of friendliness is entertaining. He showed that the deficiency of friendliness is a cold, lonely person, but an excess of friendliness is the obsequious person, who is too eager to please others. I had not thought about an excess of friendliness until I read this.

With truthfulness, Aristotle understood that the person who insists on rigid honesty at every turn might be going too far.

Shame is a quasi-virtue, which he discussed it because it lets us know when we are deficient in other, more genuine virtues. I think of it as an alarm system.

In the chapter on intellectual virtues, he examines science, art, practical wisdom (what we call common sense) and intuitive reasoning, which is also a common-sense kind of approach. These strike me more as what we think of as talents rather than virtues. This does not mean they are innate and cannot be learned, but it seems to me that folks who are very good in these areas have some kind of inherent ability they have honed. It is harder for the rest of us to become good at art, for instance. On the other hand, the common sense talent is one that seems to be acquired through experience. Maybe these intellectual virtues can be developed and encouraged, like the moral virtues. Aristotle said that intellectual virtues come from teaching but that moral virtues come from habit. We must make ourselves take on the qualities of moral excellence.

CHAPTER 3

Using ethical systems to work through a problem

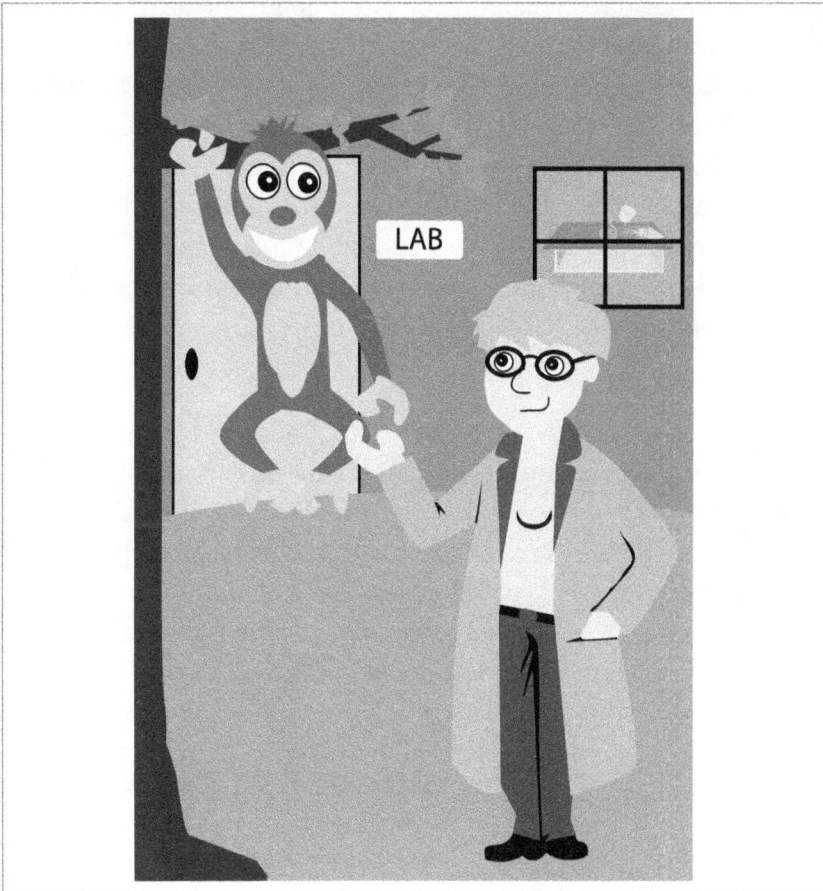

"Whose Monkey Is It, Anyway?" This was the compelling title of a 2001 episode of "Law and Order," a weekly television show drama that often takes its stories from real cases. The program is careful to run a disclaimer that says it is a work of fiction, but this is a legal protection only; many of its cases are obviously drawn from real-life stories. The case I want to discuss comes down to one of animal rights, although the episode centers around the legal responsibility of a human for the death of another human. I have not been able to confirm that this case is drawn from reality, but surely something similar has occurred somewhere. I will describe the case, then examine it from several different ethical treatments, including duty, utility, freedom and virtue ethics. We did not cover freedom ethics in the early chapters, but it is easy enough to follow here. The main question is whether animals deserve the same protection in research as humans.

The case

A researcher is found dead in his lab. There had been several monkeys in cages at the lab, and all except one are missing. The one remaining is not in its cage. The medical examiner finds a bite mark on the dead researcher that matches the bite pattern of the remaining monkey. The researcher is found to have died from an allergic reaction to the monkey's saliva. After talking with other lab employees, detectives in the case determine that a likely suspect to have let the monkeys out of their cages is a local animal rights activist. They track him down and find out that he broke into the lab and released the monkeys so that he could take them with him. The monkeys had been injected with a virus known to cause HIV and AIDS so that researchers could test cures on the monkeys. The monkeys are all under a death sentence as a result. The animal rights rescuer had wanted to take the monkeys to an environment where they could be cared for in a hospice style, rather than knowing that as they got sicker they would simply be euthanized. When he broke into the lab, he was unable to corral one of the monkeys. When the researcher arrived in the morning, the enraged monkey attacked and bit him, causing the allergic reaction that killed him (nothing about the AIDS infection killed him).

District attorneys charge the activist with second-degree manslaughter, and he refuses a plea agreement for criminally negligent homicide that would admit guilt but carry a much lower prison sentence, if any. He feels justified in refusing the plea agreement because his intention was to take the monkeys to a place that would be better for them. His intent was not to kill anyone. The death of the lab worker was purely accidental, although the prosecutor points out that the rescuer could have told someone the monkey was loose and might have prevented the lab worker's death. Even though the death was an accident as far as the rescuer is concerned, his actions did lead to that death. So in some sense, he is responsible for it.

The resolution of the case is not as important for us here as are the ways in which we look at the activist's and researchers' actions and ethical choices. Legal results do not always reflect actual justice. We will look at this case from four different ethical perspectives to see what they have to tell us about the morality of the researchers and that of the rescuer.

Duty ethics

Immanuel Kant would have us act out of right intention, regardless of the result. He also would have us act in such a way that our action can be universalized. This concept of duty is helpful in some situations. If we are not sure what to do, we can ask, "How would the world be if everyone took this action in this situation?" If the result is acceptable, the action is probably moral. If the result is not acceptable, the action is likely immoral. We believe motorists should stop at red lights. If everyone ran red lights, there would be more crashes. The idea is to see what would happen if everyone made an exception for herself: We'd have lots of crashes. So each person needs to behave in the way he or she needs everyone to behave, and not to make exceptions.

Another element of Kant's system is that good intention matters more than results. The question in the monkey case is: What is the intention of the researchers, and what is the intention of the rescuer? The researchers believe they are working toward saving human lives, and they are clearly willing to sacrifice monkey lives in this cause. I believe Kant would say in this case is that human lives are worth more than monkey lives. This stems from his consideration of humans as rational beings. Animals, by his definition, are not rational, and as such they are not capable of moral choice. Since they cannot make moral choices, they are not required to be treated as moral beings. We will see this argument again later in the chapter.

I am certain Kant would find the action of the rescuer immoral, because it involved breaking into the lab. Kant would say we should never trespass another's property, or steal, regardless of the possible results. For him, the act of stealing is always immoral. That's all there is, for him -- he does not consider the good intentions of the rescuer who is trying to make life better for other creatures. Because he was stealing someone else's property and Kant recognizes the monkeys in this case as property, the rescuer is wrong in his view.

One of the arguments used by a lawyer in this TV show case is that the rescuer was trying to defend others. The statute to which the lawyer refers was likely intended to mean other humans, but since it is not spelled out, the lawyer says it means any others. Like monkeys. The lawyers talk about the fact that 150 years ago, some humans were treated as property. Now they are not. We are on the road to stop treating monkeys and other research animals as property. It makes the prosecutor uncomfortable to think of monkeys in the same sense as human slaves, but the argument is more valid than he recognizes. The issue of what may constitute property is significant, and undergoes constant revision. Even landed property concepts are changeable: We go out of our way to preserve some pieces of land rather than develop them, and we sometimes try to return pieces of land to the descendants of their original owners.

Property is not an easy idea, and the notion of owning another creature is not simple. I pay a city tax on my cat, but I hardly think of myself as owning her. We have a relationship far richer than many I have with other people. I think of myself as intellectually superior to her, but she is better at some other things than I am, such as stalking bugs and smelling diverse smells. We both do what we do and leave the property rights argument to someone else.

Utility ethics

Early utilitarians, especially Jeremy Bentham, might say that anything that increases pleasure for humans and decreases pain for humans is the action to choose. I think he would probably approve of medical research that promises to prolong life for humans, even at the cost of animal lives and freedom. Bentham did publish comments on animal rights at one point -- his *Introduction to the Principles of Morals and Legislation*, while not disputing that animals are rightful property of humans, said that they should not be subjected to unnecessary suffering. He said the issue is not whether animals can reason but whether they can feel pain. He predicted that legislation would eventually extend to protect "everything that breathes." His calculation of pleasure and pain had room in it for the suffering of animals. Perhaps he understood that when we cause animal suffering, it causes us pain as well -- maybe not specific pain, but certainly long-lasting social pain. Although Bentham wanted to prevent animal suffering, he would not do so at the cost of human suffering.

Other utilitarians understand, even more so, that living in a society in which we trade one life for another is not good for the long-term health of the society. John Stuart Mill is in this category. He would claim that an action that sacrifices animal lives decreases human pleasure and increases human pain, regardless of the capacity of the animal to feel pleasure or pain. Contemporary utilitarian Peter Singer would agree with Mill but would add that the animal's capacity for pain should be considered. Singer would even go so far as to say that some animals are more capable of pain than some humans, especially if the humans in question had diminished mental capacity. This argument of his has sparked controversy but it bears consideration. I believe he makes it not to diminish the value we place on human life but to increase the value we place on animal life. Later I will suggest that perhaps we place too much value on human life, and that this overemphasis twists our choices to extremes we might be better off avoiding.

As to the morality of the rescuer's actions in our legal case, the utilitarian's evaluation might stem from his perspective on the researcher's morality. Because Bentham would approve of the research that would promote pleasure in human lives, he would disapprove of the rescuer taking the monkeys. Because Mill and Singer would disapprove of the research, they would salute the rescuer as someone trying to restore equilibrium or put things back where they ought to be to ensure the greatest good for the greatest number of people. Using utility ethics makes us want to quantify things, and some things -- such as respect for others and to whom we should give it -- are difficult to quantify.

Freedom ethics

Jean-Paul Sartre and other existentialists say that we must act so as to will ourselves free, and to will others free as well. We must also take responsibility for our actions -- we might say we should "own" them.

From this angle, the researchers might be justified in taking the lives of other creatures, if they do so out of a thoughtful understanding that they are making a moral decision. Sartre might say that a researcher's choice to use monkeys as subjects without their consent is acceptable as long as the researcher understands and takes responsibility for ending the life of another. I'm not sure this is a valid argument because the monkeys are not allowed to choose, and because the basis of freedom ethics is the access of all participants to choose their own path. Besides, in the case of monkeys, they may very well be able to make moral choices and we just don't know it yet. If we are willing others free so that we may be free, we must will the monkeys free because we have no right to cage them.

As for the rescuer, a freedom ethicist would salute his willingness to accept responsibility for his actions in court, even though he did not anticipate the death of the lab worker. The ultimate test of an existentialist is his willingness to stand up for his choices regardless of the result. The notion of freedom ethics might also support the idea of the monkeys being unrestricted, if they are seen as thinking creatures.

Virtue ethics

Aristotle would have us shape a character and state of soul such that when a moment of choice arrives, we will know the right thing to do out of that good character. Qualities we cultivate to form that character include things like courage, wisdom and appropriate pride and temper. Courage allows us to follow through on a difficult choice such as stopping animal research when we believe it to be wrong, even though it means delaying results for humans. Wisdom helps us arrive at an understanding of why much animal research is wrong, especially when we give animals a disease or deformity in order to test cures or fixes. We would never do that to human subjects; what makes us think it's all right to do so to animals? One day there may be an accounting, and we will be found woefully short in our treatment of our fellow creatures. Appropriate pride encourages us to strive to be better people, which might lead us to see that animal research in most cases is unnecessary and wrong. Appropriate temper was the most revealing of Aristotle's virtues, for me, because I came to understand that there are times when it's right to be outraged about something. There are moments when we should allow our passions to be expressed, when we see injustices that need to be righted. A researcher operating from this ethic would not perform animal research except in very specific situations, certainly not on the wide scale that is done now and even more that was done until recent legislation made it more difficult.

How would Aristotle view the rescuer who broke into the lab? Certainly he shows courage of an appropriate amount, knowing that he may be caught and punished. Wisdom leads him to see that the research being conducted in that lab is unjust. Appropriate pride makes him think he is the right one to mount the rescue. Appropriate temper is what fuels his desire to see the monkeys freed. He shows us what a virtuous person is about.

The numbers

According to The Center for Laboratory Animal Welfare, about 25 million animals are under experiment in the United States (about 100 million worldwide). The center says that roughly 60% of animals used in research are for biomedical purposes, 17% for testing drugs and vaccines, 5% for testing consumer products, and less than 10% for education. The animals used in education include school dissections and veterinary school practice, although Tufts Veterinary School recently stopped using healthy dogs for such purposes. Imagine a school taking a healthy animal and breaking its leg so a student can practice setting it! But that is hardly different from what drug researchers do, which is to give animals a disease so they can study responses to varying treatments. They would never do this to humans, so what justifies doing it to animals who cannot give consent? If any population is vulnerable, it is captive animals.

My second-year biology class in high school performed 10 dissections. I believe there is indeed value in students getting their hands on actual tissue. Now, some veterinary students can use artificial animal tissue to practice suturing, and there are remarkable computer simulations and plastic models of everything we used to have to handle in person. Schools do not have to continue using actual animals. We dissected Jackson sharks, fetal pigs and turtles, none of which necessarily was a unique learning experience that could not now be duplicated with models.

I particularly remember the day we did live chickens. The teacher went to great length to explain that these chickens were all sick and would have been put to death in any case, so they might as well be used for something educational. He killed them as we watched. He used a tool called a pith, which is essentially a piece of metal shaped like a pencil but not quite so sharp at the end. He inserted it into the back of their necks and hit it with a little hammer, which separated their spinal cords from their brains. From then on we knew they did not feel pain. But it is true that chickens are still active, "running around with their heads cut off." Their nervous systems stay active for several minutes, and in fact after one of them stopped flopping around, the teacher jump-started its heart with a couple of electrical probes. That experience was compelling, far more than the dissections on already-dead animals.

If we had dissected cats, I could not have participated. I saw a photograph in *USA Today* on Oct. 28, 2003, illustrating a story about SARS and how it was being passed around in Asian markets. The photo showed cats in a crate in a marketplace, waiting to be sold as food. They were still alive, jammed into that crate. They could not move. I was physically sick for three days, as the photo kept returning to me. I understood intellectually that those were not someone's pets, that they were feral, and that being someone's dinner was a natural part of the cycle of life in that part of the world. But to come home to my own cat and see those others in my imagination was more than I could bear for several days.

The reaction to that photograph, by me and by others, helps justify that the number of animals being used for testing consumer products is dwindling -- as manufacturers find that people are uncomfortable knowing their shampoo was tested by being dripped into a bunny's eyes to see how long it would take for their eyes to burn, or worse. Also, by now most of the major active ingredients in consumer products have been tested. There is no point in repeating research.

Animals are used to test drugs because the Unites States Food and Drug Administration and other national organizations require that a drug be tested on animals before it is tested on humans. Scientists are developing alternative testing methods that will one day make this policy unnecessary. Such alternatives include computer simulations and tissue tests, in which a reaction may be tested on voluntarily donated human tissue rather than on a captive animal. The results are more useful in most cases because some drugs do not react in some animals the same way as in humans, so they need to be tested on humans regardless.

Why we're in this mess

Homo sapiens may be intellectually superior to most of Earth's other animal species, but that does not make us more worthy of respect. We may think we need to get a certain amount of protein from other animals, but that hardly gives us license to use them as test subjects for the preservation of our own species. And what is it about that species preservation impulse that we are so desperate to prolong human life at nearly any expense? The answer is not that it is simply human nature. Eastern cultures, as well as Native American cultures, are willing to embrace whatever time we have and not fear what comes later. Many social groups of humans have not and do not find it necessary to extend individual lives beyond their normal course; contemporary Western societies are the exception rather than the rule when we consider humanity over the centuries.

So to say that we take extreme measures to prolong human life is not an exaggeration. Those measures include sacrificing animal lives in pursuit of remedies for our own ailments. We rarely, if ever, experiment on animals to find cures for animal diseases. Even though this means we are using them as a means to our own ends, Kant would excuse this behavior because he would say most animals do not meet his definition of rational creatures. Because animals lack an awareness of time and an ability to differentiate between what we think of as right and wrong, they are not subject to his morality. They are not moral beings themselves, and as such, humans are excused from treating them with the same respect they owe other humans. I think he is wrong.

Bentham, Mill and Singer agree we should not cause animals unnecessary suffering. Singer in particular argues that animals are grossly mistreated by humans at nearly every turn. I think he is right.

I think Sartre does not care one way or another about animals, unless they are able to make choices. I think if he had ever had a pet cat he would understand that they do make choices. He makes no comment, that I can find. I think he is neither right nor wrong.

Aristotle defined a horse as a thing that fulfilled a horselike role. Whichever horse best fit that description, of a thing with a long tail and four legs and short hair that runs well and sleeps standing up, that was the best horse. The job description of a horse in nature does not include having stuff dripped into its eyes to see how much it takes to make them burn. It does not include the administration of medications so that humans can see how they affect the heart rate of the horse. The function of a horse is apparent, and when we twist that function, we change our own nature for the worse. I think Aristotle is right.

We have no reason to think we can manipulate other living creatures for our own ends. Imagine if one day beings from another world began research on us -- then maybe we will understand the harm we have caused.

CHAPTER 4

Let's Get Focused

In this chapter, I'll tell you about the modern versions of some of the early virtues. These four are most important to me: courage, generosity, authenticity, and an appropriate self-image.

Courage

We talked in Chapter 2 about Aristotle's definition of courage, a virtue on a spectrum between cowardice and foolhardiness. Courage is not the absence of fear; it is a willingness to take action in spite of our fear. We use courage to make ourselves tackle a challenge, whether it is one bold action or a new habit.

We have a tendency to resist change, based on a fear of failure at something new. Striking out in new directions does not always come naturally to adults, although it does seem to be a natural tendency in infants and young children. Maybe we evolve into non-risk-takers because our environments teach us not to explore too much, that there's danger out there. Maybe our caretakers overprotect us due to their own fears of danger. For whatever reasons, too many of us grow into people who are afraid to risk failure or rejection. So we leave things alone, knowing our situation is flawed, but too fearful of the potential negative consequences to risk making a change. We develop strategies to avoid those fears. One day we realize we can throw away those strategies, because the thing we were afraid of is not so bad anymore. Or maybe we just decide to try something in spite of the fear. That's an invigorating feeling.

These moments when we close our eyes and leap from a cliff require courage. I'm reminded of a leadership-building exercise in which my coworkers and I had opportunities to navigate a rope course 15 feet above the ground, rappel from a three-story tower, and for the final activity, climb a 12-foot pole and jump about three feet to a trapeze bar. Everyone did the rope course; we were matched up with buddies and the fear factor was minimal. About six of us rappelled; once you swung yourself out of the window to begin the descent, the actual walk down the building was simple. That moment of fear just before you let go, though, was too overwhelming for three or four people, who made it to the top of the tower but then backed out.

The most significant moment for me, though, was during the final activity. We climbed a telephone pole with spikes in its sides, stood on top of it, and then had to jump about three feet to grab a metal bar, after which we would be lowered to the ground. The climb was easy, even though there was an awkward moment climbing around our own hips to be able to stand on top of the pole. Then came that last moment of decision in which we each had to make ourselves take the leap. Three feet doesn't seem like much; the bar was just far enough away that you had to jump. I stood up there for a good minute and a half, trying to breathe slowly and muster up the courage to make the jump. The first four people who'd gone had been a little scared, but they had managed to climb and jump quickly just to get it over with. Two men, then two women. It was up to me to finish the day by impressing everyone with how courageous the girls were.

We each wore a rock climbing harness in case of a fall; the facilitator took up most of the slack in the line so he could catch anyone who made an accidental slip. Finally, I realized that to overcome the fear of jumping, all I needed was to ask the same question that had allowed me to make other advances in other places in life: "What is the worst thing that could happen if I do this?" In this particular case, the worst thing that could happen was that I could jump and miss the bar, and the facilitator would lower me to the ground dangling from the harness instead of from the bar. Once I thought about the worst-case scenario, my choice was not so hard. I was still afraid, but now I could do it because I knew that that absolute worst possible outcome wasn't all that bad in the grand scheme of things. So I did it. After standing there on top of that pole far longer than anyone else, I did it.

The experience itself wasn't particularly "fun," or had any great payoff, but there were two rewards. The first was immediate, a sense of confidence that came from knowing I had overcome a challenge. We get this feeling from all sorts of places in life if we welcome opportunities to master obstacles. The second reward from my jump came a half hour later, in the debriefing after the day's activities. Each of us was asked to describe something we'd learned that day. Most folks talked about understanding the value of good communication from the day's early exercises; a few talked about how neat it was to see even more women doing some of the activities than the men. The last speaker was one of my female coworkers (one of the three of us who'd done all the challenges), who surprised me by saying that she most appreciated watching me struggle with my fear on top of that pole. She said she'd thought I would have jumped immediately without worry, and that seeing me have to stand there and overcome a fear revealed two things to her: that I was indeed afraid of some things, and the one that gave me goose bumps -- seeing me overcome a fear in a public setting like that made her realize what courage was all about.

I don't know about all that, but I've never forgotten my own response to that fear, or her response to seeing it worked out. Ever since then, it's been a little easier to choose a leap into the unknown, because I have the memory of having done it once. Ever since then I've had a little more patience with people who are struggling with making a change in their lives, or with trying to decide how best to solve a problem. We are indeed afraid of change, but we can assuage that fear by testing its limits as often as necessary. The more times we fling ourselves off the top of a pole, the easier it gets.

Choosing to change a situation is most difficult the first few times we try, but the more tests we face, the easier it becomes to pass them. The choice may be to improve a work or family situation, to leave an abusive spouse, to claim a legal right of access for a civil opportunity, or even to pack up and leave a home to pursue life elsewhere. The choices are seldom easy, especially at first, but we must make them when the rewards are worth the risks.

Sometimes we make those choices even when the risks outweigh the reward -- the true acts of courage. Packing up your children and leaving a spouse, knowing that you may be pursued, harassed or even killed, is not a simple choice. This is the sort of choice many people face, most of them women whose options are often limited by external factors. These include the possible reactions of the jealous mate and the economic hardships of striking out on one's own. The hardest part of the equation, though, is the fear built in to the act of making this choice. This sort of choice is hardly one for which we can practice. We are hard-pressed to gradually make riskier choices, as I was able to do on the day I jumped from the pole. I had the chance to spend the day working up to that moment; most of the people in the abusive spouse situation have one chance, one perfect or imperfect moment that must be seized or lost forever. We can understand why so often people in this situation can't muster up the nerve to escape the bad situation.

As moral beings who want to be agents of change for the good, we can only help others see their own potential; we can't make their choices for them. As the cowardly lion discovered when he met the Wizard of Oz, courage is not something we can be given. We have it inside us all along and have only to act on it to bring it to life.

Courage, Part II

Until I did some reading about Jackie Robinson a few years ago, I'd always been peripherally aware of the courage and patience he practiced in 1946 and 1947, the latter when he broke major league baseball's color barrier. He played a season of minor league ball for Montreal in 1946. Now that I've done some more thorough reading on the subject, I'm even more impressed with the willingness of his first boss to take the steps required to make it all happen. Jules Tygiel's *Baseball's Great Experiment: Jackie Robinson and His Legacy* tells how the Brooklyn Dodgers' Branch Rickey spent three years planning and scheming to set the stage and choose the right athlete. Many observers agree that he chose exactly and only the right one, and that if he'd been wrong, it would have set back integration in baseball for probably another seven or eight years.

Rickey understood the resistance of most of the people involved. He agreed to arrange trades for some of his Southern-raised players who couldn't make themselves adapt, and he didn't think they were bad people. He knew they weren't going to be able to overcome their lifelong prejudices, and as long as they behaved professionally, he was willing to give them a way out.

Rickey's story is nearly as inspiring as Robinson's in many respects. His rebellion against most of the other team executives put him on nearly as lonely a spot as Robinson. Only one other team official, Bill Veeck of the Cleveland Indians, agreed that an enormous amount of talent was being overlooked in the Negro Leagues and was willing to do something about it. After Rickey and Robinson got the process started, Veeck chose Larry Doby, a Negro League player in New York who was originally from South Carolina to become the American League's first African-American player. His early career with the Indians was very successful; he was the heavy-hitting hero of more than one World Series.

1948 brought more Negro League stars for Rickey's project: Roy Campanella and Don Newcombe. Throughout this process, Rickey's interviews with his potential pioneers always stressed the importance of the players behaving in particular ways. They played their games very well and kept their mouths shut -- for a while, anyway. By mid-1948, Robinson had had enough of patience, and he began answering ignorant questions of the press with the scorn they deserved. Not only did he begin to stand up for himself, he did so without consulting Rickey. His emancipation was complete.

Looking back at this part of our history reveals the complexity of the dynamic of freedom. Jackie Robinson had been an army lieutenant during World War II and had represented his school in several intercollegiate sports; he didn't see why he couldn't do anything anyone else could do. When an opportunity for emancipation was offered to him, he took it. In spite of the abuse he knew he would suffer and did suffer, he leaped at the chance to do something important for himself and all other athletes in his position. Rickey's and Veeck's stories are nearly as admirable; they knew the abuse they would take and they took it. Their speeches said that they were just looking for ways to make their clubs better, but that can't have been their only motivation. Deep down they knew that someone had to be the first to effect social change, and they were willing to take on the challenge.

Courage, Part III

A friend sent me a contest in which a television network would help you make a dream come true. I constructed a plan that would allow me to be a bullpen catcher for a day at a local minor-league park. It was something I'd always thought would be fun and help a team but not put me in the spotlight. I was starting to set up the video to send to the network. Then I got a new CD with a favorite singer doing a remake of a classic. I loved that he had not changed the instrumentation very much, that his rendition was powerful and spiritual, and that it was everything

I liked about the original song. I was singing it in the car with him at the top of my lungs, crying. Suddenly I realized I didn't want to be a bullpen catcher at a baseball game. I wanted to sing the national anthem.

I will not attend a game unless I can get there in time for the anthem. The game is incomplete without it. It doesn't matter if it's instrumental or vocal, poorly rendered or amazing, or somewhere in between. It is a necessary part of the experience for me. There is something about acknowledging our attachment to our nation that makes sport complete for me. I cannot imagine sport without such an allegiance. It is not a blind patriotism that says that anything my country does is OK, but it is an acknowledgement that even with our faults, we strive for something noble. This is true for many nations. Their anthems express the wish for nobility, or the allegiance to a homeland, that gives sport an extra richness.

I realized that I remembered some national anthems better than I did some games. I remember one game especially, a Carolina Panthers NFL game in late August, 1997. It was the first game of the season, at home against the Washington Redskins. The stadium public-address announcer said to rise for the national anthem, to be sung by Gary Morris. My heart stopped for a second. I'd spent the previous few years listening to a cast recording of *Les Miserables*, with Morris doing the lead vocal. He came up as a country singer, but then he showed his talent doing one of the more challenging roles in musical theater. I adored his voice. And now he was going to sing "The Star-Spangled Banner" at a football game I was attending. When he sang the first line, I was already crying. It was glorious. He had the perfect tone, the perfect everything. Often I sing along if invited, but this time I could not begin to interfere with that voice. When he finished, I nearly left the stadium. I did not care who won that game. My experience was complete.

Several years later, I was singing along with Clay Aiken's "Bridge Over Troubled Water" and realized I wanted to sing the national anthem at a baseball game. Then I realized I didn't want to sing one national anthem. I wanted to sing two. I've heard "O Canada" at some baseball games, and I especially remember hearing it several times in the early 1990s when the Toronto Blue Jays played twice in the World Series. My favorite rendition was by an *a capella* group called The Nylons, who opened one of the games with it. I could not see the game because I was working, but I heard it on the radio and thought it was amazing.

My local minor-league team, the Charlotte Knights, is in the International League, so-called because it used to include a Canadian team. I checked the schedule to see when that team would be visiting and asked my mother if she would sing with me. She has a lead vocalist kind of voice and has had training. Mine is the sort of voice best used doing harmony, which is how we set it up. We started rehearsing in earnest about two weeks before the public tryout. One day we had walked a few miles and then rehearsed, and we recorded ourselves. I sounded really terrible, which I later realized was due to the walking. I began to feel afraid we would sound awful at the audition.

As it approached I relaxed a little, reminding myself that the worst-case scenario was not that bad. If we were bad, they just wouldn't ask us to sing at a game. Only a few people would be at the park when we auditioned, and no one would know who we were. The risk was small, except to my pride. When the day came, we drove to the ballpark, singing both anthems five times on the way. As we came from the parking lot and approached the stadium, we could hear someone on the public address system singing. She was not good. After hearing three people try it and none of them do so well, I felt better about our chances.

We wrote down contact information, and I asked if the staff needed people to do "O Canada" when the Ottawa Lynx visited. The lead woman's eyes lit up. She said they always have trouble finding people to do that. Apparently not that many people know the words. I had counted on that as a hook, and said so. She liked that. Then we sang a few bars, and my dad pointed out that the microphone was not turned on. He's very helpful about stuff like that. The woman fixed it, and we started again. "O Canada" went great. I'd quit trying to do harmony, and just sang it straight with Mom, sometimes an octave down. We'd agreed she would start the first two lines of "The Star-Spangled Banner" and then I'd come in on the harmony, and that's what happened. I do a thing that's sort of a combination of the bass and the tenor, which I knew after the tryout I'd have two months to nail perfectly.

After we got done the three officials clapped and said, "We will definitely call you for the Ottawa series." So that was it. I was not as terrified when we were singing as I'd thought I would be, although I picked a seat and looked mostly at it the whole time. With sunglasses on, who knows the difference?

The team called a few days later and scheduled us for a game in June. Mom and I each sang "O Canada" once a day for two months, and a week before the game, we met a few times to sing it together. We were scheduled for a Thursday night game, the second of a four-game series. I was no longer afraid because we had already passed the tough test of the audition. I knew we would be fine at the game.

I got home the Tuesday night before the Thursday game, and there was a message from the team asking if we could fill in on Wednesday at the day game. We did it and videotaped ourselves, which allowed us to fine-tune some presentation details for the big game on Thursday. Both games went great. Several of our friends came to the night game, and we sounded pretty good. We honored Canada and America, and we didn't go flat or mispronounce the words or do any of the stuff singers worry about. Once I made up my mind to do it, the whole thing seemed to go as if it had been scripted. Even the surprise of being called for the extra game turned out to be a blessing, as we were able to tweak a few things to make it all sound even better.

The point of this is to choose something you want to do but are afraid to try, and then do it. Just do it. This is how we become courageous people, by doing courageous things. At some point we realize that courage is a virtue we can develop in ourselves. We can go through life afraid, or we can learn not to take ourselves so seriously. We risk rejection every day. Sometimes it happens and sometimes it doesn't. The lesson is that we become better people by asking ourselves to be courageous.

Generosity

To be generous means to think of someone else. In some moral or ethical systems, being generous means thinking of someone else at the expense of yourself, but I will not ask that of you. It makes us feel good to help others or to make them happy, and I believe there is nothing wrong with that. Some of us have grown up in systems in which we are expected to be totally selfless. I'm not sure that's feasible. There are rare occasions when we make sacrifices for others in which we are not doing it for our own good feeling, so it is possible to be that selfless. We see it when parents lay down their lives for their children, or soldiers knowingly put themselves in danger to protect others. This is both courage and generosity, but I don't know that it is workable in everyday life.

In duty ethics, Kant would have us be wary of doing good for another for any reason than duty and a moral imperative. He warned that such acts are not moral because they have an ulterior motive, which is the good feeling we get. Kant thought we should do good only because it is good. Joseph Butler, an English bishop writing in the eighteenth century, said that human nature is to love ourselves. He reassured us that we can recognize that aiding others makes us feel good, and that this is indeed part of our nature. Don't be alarmed by this self-love idea; it is only acknowledging the way we are. Sometimes we try so hard to think of others that we forget to think of ourselves. True self-love must, by definition, include love of others, and connecting with others and doing good for them are some of the ways in which we gain happiness. A life without such connections is empty. It may include other pleasures, but these are uniquely human pleasures that can be reached no other way. Butler explains that simply not harming our neighbor is not enough; we must actively promote the neighbor's good "to consider ourselves as having a real share in his happiness." (*Three Sermons*, 59) He understands that we cannot affect the whole universe with our benevolence -- that role is reserved for a divinity. We must figure out who our neighbor is, and then love our neighbor as we do ourselves. Our neighbors are the people with whom we come in contact, not the entire world. Butler would not have us try to save everyone, only to be good to those we can affect.

This idea of self-love was tough for me, because I thought it meant too much self-interest. But once I saw Butler's claim that this is our nature and we might as well work with it instead of fighting it, it's the kind of love of others that works very well. We do good things for other people because it makes us feel good, and that's fine. The other person benefits in either case -- and in time, I think maybe we rely less and less on the good feeling, and we still do the good for others without expecting the reward. Benevolence, in fact, furthers our self-love, because doing kindnesses for others makes us feel good. You've heard of hedonism, in which the object is pleasure -- Butler agrees that an interest in pleasure motivates many of our actions. His belief that we gain pleasure by helping others does not so much clash with hedonism as it adds a dimension to it. The real hedonists understood that long-term pleasure brings more happiness than short-term pleasure. Doing good for others, over time, adds up to the best long-term pleasure there is.

What are some types of generosity? You can be generous with money, time or energy. If you have money, parting with it for a worthy cause is pretty easy, especially once you get some practice. It is harder when you are giving up money you could use for yourself, but this gift means even more. The world probably runs on donations made by the wealthy. But maybe the small donations made by the rest of us, that came from some sacrifice, provide the good energy that makes things happen. For most causes, volunteer time is far more important than money. Cash buys material and equipment, but people distribute and maintain it. People donate blood, pick up trash, and cook food in homeless shelters. Cash can only purchase so much blood for transfusions. At some point, people must donate it, or we run out. Possibly a machine can pick up roadside trash, but someone still has to operate that machine. More often, people do the picking up themselves. Somebody must collect, wash and mend the clothing given to a shelter, and then decide how to distribute it.

Only people can teach other people how to read. Only people can take the dog for a walk and throw her a tennis ball. Only people can clean up the litter from a neighbor's yard after a creek floods. Only people can drive you around town the first time you visit, and show you how great it is. Twice I've visited cities I thought I would hate. Because an acquaintance (later a friend) stepped up to provide a tour, I was able to see those cities through their eyes. I appreciated both trips far more than if my friends had not played tour guide. Cash can buy some of these things, but people who give them freely change the nature of the experience.

My favorite definition of love comes from science fiction writer Robert Heinlein, who said that love is the state in which your happiness is more important to me than my own. It means that I will think of your needs before I satisfy my own. Generosity is a little bit like love in this way. Being generous means that we take care of the other person before we take care of ourselves. This does not mean that we turn ourselves into doormats and never pay attention to ourselves. It means that we can give of our time and energy to other people, because we know it will benefit them as well as us.

Authenticity

The two most important characteristics I look for in friends is that they be genuine, and that they not take themselves too seriously. These are the last two virtues in this chapter. One we will call authenticity, and the other we will call pride. Pride has gotten a bad reputation, but we will define it so that it makes sense as a virtue.

Being authentic means being true and taking responsibility for all your actions and choices. It means that you do not rely on others to tell you what to do, or blame them when something goes wrong. The hardest thing about authenticity is that not only do we not deceive others, but we do not deceive ourselves. In the contemporary world, we have learned so many ways to trick ourselves that sometimes we lose sight of who we are. Being authentic means that we will be honest with ourselves -- not only when it is painful, but especially when it is painful. It is not enough to be virtuous when it is easy.

Learning to be genuine is challenging. This is the hardest of these four virtues -- to re-invent yourself as an authentic, honest, unflinching person. From this virtue, the others come more easily. Once you stop lying to yourself and to others, becoming courageous and generous and appropriately proud comes easily from the state of soul you have created.

The school of philosophy that most appeals to authenticity is called existentialism. It arose in Europe about a hundred years ago and reached its highest popularity in France, during and after World War II. People there felt anguished about the way the world was turning out, and they found this approach to be a good way to explain things. The gimmick is that existentialists say we can't explain anything, and that nothing in life has any meaning unless we decide it does. Because people got to choose, they could choose to disbelieve the Nazis, and believe that the worldview of supremacy was wrong.

Then and now, being authentic means you get to decide what has meaning for you. You do not have to ask other people to make rules for you. You can reject cultural mores that you think are silly or unnecessary. You can create a code of conduct for yourself that is based on what you believe is right, not on the worry of getting caught doing something society thinks is wrong. Just because a group thinks something is wrong does not mean the group knows what it is talking about. Once you begin to rely on your own good judgment, you begin to see that some of the ideas that social groups hold important really are not. Worries about fashion restrictions, which sport to play if you are a boy or a girl, what job you should be in if you are from a particular family ... all of this is irrelevant and not worthy of your energy. As you become an authentic person, you find that you are not so interested in what the group says. You are more interested in equal access for jobs and recreational activities, regardless of the kind of person who is participating. You find that you are concerned with ideas about justice, regardless of the rules in place.

Becoming a genuine person will make you feel much better than fitting in with the crowd. It makes you feel strong and confident to know that you do not rely on the group's opinion to form your own.

Becoming genuine allows you to put your energy into places it can be well spent, rather than wasting it on worrying about what other people think of you.

Becoming genuine means you will always acknowledge your actions, choices and decisions. You will never blame someone else for your mistakes. You will say that you chose those deeds, and you will take responsibility for any bad results. You will mean this. It will flow from you naturally because once you have become an authentic person, you would not ever think of trying to shove off your problems on someone else. You will never imagine trying to evade responsibility for anything you did. You will do the best you can at the time, and later you will acknowledge your decision. You will not take on someone else's problem unless you choose to do so; you will never again do a task solely because it is expected of you. For your honesty, you will respect yourself, and the world will respect you.

President Harry Truman had a sign on his desk that stated, "The buck stops here." He understood that all decisions made by his administration were ultimately his responsibility. He was willing to take the heat for the bad choices and the congratulations for the good ones. He made one of the most difficult decisions by a world leader after being in office for only a few months. He had to decide whether to use an atomic bomb on his country's enemy. Believing that using the atomic bomb would save lives on both sides over the course of the war, he chose to use it. He is one of the most respected presidents because he knew the consequences of his decision and he had the courage to stand behind it. Many people disagreed with his decision, but few called him a coward or anything but honest and genuine.

I am not saying that in order to be genuine, you have to always be making bold choices. It is in the everyday choices that we create virtues, which includes authenticity. This quality is linked with courage. It takes courage to stand on your own and not follow the herd. It takes an act of will to separate yourself from a group when you think the group is wrong. You find that after several instances of making these choices, it is not quite so difficult as when you started.

Creating an authentic person takes time. We have a great deal of socialization to overcome. We have many messages from our culture that we must disregard. This takes time. It does not happen overnight. Once you make the decision to build a genuine person, though, the transformation begins right away. It is thrilling to watch yourself stepping out of old habits and old beliefs. It is exciting to see yourself choosing an activity because you know it is good for you, and not because it is popular. The possibilities are wide open once you stop wondering what the group thinks is best.

I am not asking you to reject every value you have been taught. After examining those values, you will conclude that many of them feel right, that they are rooted in goodness and in treating each other with respect. The important step is to examine those values for yourself and not to just accept what you've been told. The beliefs you question and then accept will be much stronger than those you only accept.

Appropriate Self-Image

We talked about pride in Chapter 2, where I explained some of Aristotle's virtues. A few hundred years after Aristotle, some of the early Christians believed that pride was a vice. What we must do here is distinguish appropriate pride from the inappropriate kinds. Then we'll know we are on the right track with the right kind of pride. We'll know it is a virtue, a legitimate part of the kind of character we are trying to build.

I mentioned these definitions quickly in Chapter 2, but now we will go into them more thoroughly. I am using ideas from Richard Taylor's "The Virtue of Pride," an essay that helped me understand these distinctions.

Pride is the appropriate appreciation you have for your own goodness. This means that you are good, that you see that you are good, and you wish to continue being good. You are proud of the character you have created, and you desire it to continue. This is a self-fulfilling motivation. We like the way we feel when we act out of good intentions and good motivations, so we want to keep feeling that way. Pride is what psychologists might call positive reinforcement. The reward of good feeling makes us want to keep repeating the actions and thoughts that bring it to us. From this virtue flows the virtue of generosity, which we talked about earlier in this chapter. When you are generous with others, you feel good inside. This is the same kind of feeling as with pride. As long as your appreciation of your goodness is appropriate, you're in good shape.

There are three ways, which I will call regions, in which we can make mistakes with pride. We can feel too little pride, we can feel pride about an improper action or quality, or we can rely on others to feel pride for us. Many people are in these regions and will be happier once they find their way to the region of appropriate pride.

Those who do not feel enough pride in themselves might be called self-abasing, or people with low self-esteem. Esteem is the quality a group has for someone it believes will help the group. Self-esteem is the same feeling, an understanding of your value, but it is sometimes harder to see a quality in ourselves that we see in others. There are lots of people who help the group but do not recognize this. They do not have much pride in their accomplishments, even though it would be acceptable and even correct for them to feel it. If you know one of these people, perhaps you have tried to point out a laudable deed or quality in your friend, only to have her downplay it or say it is not worth mentioning. It is a very difficult chore to get a person to understand his own worth. This is a feeling that might be kindled by another person, but must grow inside the good person. At some point, each of us must recognize our own goodness and freely salute it. That is the right kind of pride, which keeps us going on the path of goodness.

The next region of pride where we can mess up is called egotism. This is the kind of pride Paul was talking about in early Christianity, which he said could lead to a fall. Destructive pride is mentioned even earlier in Judeo-Christian literature, in *The Book of Proverbs*. This is the kind of feeling about yourself that is not appropriate, because the feeling does not fit the quality. One example might be of a salesman who thinks he is very good at his work, but at the end of the day, he has only made a lot of contacts and has not sold any product. His pride in his ability to talk to people and get their phone numbers will not be appropriate if a few days later those contacts do not result in any sales. Arthur Miller's *Death of a Salesman* is about such a man. Willy Loman believes himself to be a good salesman, but he is not, and he cannot see this about himself.

Another example of improper pride could be a musical entertainer. Some popular music stars have good looks and nice clothes, but not necessarily very good singing voices. It is almost funny to hear of singers who grow so enchanted with their popularity that they forget they have little talent.

We see examples of unsuitable pride in all sorts of leaders. Some political leaders have talents that get them into their positions, but some of them become so enamored of their positions and their power that they fail to do their jobs. They expend more energy on keeping their jobs than on doing their jobs. This fixation on the trappings of an office is not the right kind of pride.

These kinds of egotism are also called arrogance. Arrogance includes the people who think they are better than others when they aren't. It also includes people who think they are better than others but who should not feel that way because it is dangerous. We are not to compare ourselves to others but to our internal standards of excellence.

The third kind of wrongful appreciation of goodness is vanity, in which we become overly concerned with what other people think of us. This can be mixed in with egotism, especially if you are a rock star and you believe there is some good reason lots of fans adore you. After a bit, you begin to believe the hype. This kind of pride is common among many American teenagers, who spend lots of time worrying about what others think of them. Once you become a cool kid, you spend lots of energy keeping up whatever character got you there -- which means pandering to the opinions of others. As long as the other kids think you are good, everything is fine. Once they turn against you, you are in trouble because your self-image had been based on their opinions.

All three of these kinds of wrongful pride have a price. Those who feel they are not worthy of pride may never see themselves as the good people they are. Those who think they are better than they are may never learn to correct their flaws. Those who depend on the opinions of others may never learn to think for themselves.

The right kind of pride is the way to happiness. It is not vain or pompous. It rarely considers itself, but when it does, there is a calm pat on the back. Patting yourself on the back now and then is a great idea, especially if it means you will not go around looking for others to do it for you.

CHAPTER 5

Embracing the Change

"If you want to be somebody else, change your mind."

Composer: Ken Block, Artist: Sister Hazel

We get to choose what kind of people we will be. How exciting is that? You are not resigned to stay the same person you have always been. You can transform yourself. You don't have to wait for someone else to tell you what to do; you get to decide what to do and what kind of person you want to be.

I hope that having read this far, you have decided you want to be a person of virtue. You want to construct the kind of character that makes being good come naturally. You want to shape yourself into a person who knows the right thing to do and does it, and for whom doing good is not tortuous. You want to be the person for whom doing good is just what you do.

You may be surprised by how simple this process is. There are two components to it, and you can manage them both. I can't say what percentage of the transformation comes from each of the two elements, but it doesn't matter. You have to do them both, and once you do them both, you're done. One of them is an ongoing process, so maybe in that sense you are never done. But it's not complicated. It may not be easy, but it is not complicated.

Component 1: Believe that being virtuous is a worthwhile target, and believe you will do it.

Component 2: Practice.

That's it. Believe in being good, then practice being good. I'll help with some details, but that's pretty much it. The trick is to realize that we are concerned with the process, not the product. We are making ourselves into people of virtue, which requires daily effort.

Like any endeavor, you must want to do it, and you must practice doing it -- such as learning to play tennis, or the piano. It really is that simple. Once you believe a thing is good, you must put that belief into practice with daily action. If you do not act on a belief, you don't completely believe it. American thinker William James said that a little over a hundred years ago. He said we make habits out of ideas we believe to be right. We put things into practice. Nike should pay him for the "Just Do It" slogan. He said when you believe deep down, you will put whatever it is into practice. The reverse is true for some things, too, like brushing our teeth and holding doors open for others; we put an idea into practice first, and over time we come to believe in it.

A friend of mine realized he was in lousy shape, even though round is a shape. He wanted to become a runner again, as he had been in his 20s. He could barely walk to the end of his driveway before getting out of breath. Six months later, he ran a 5K. A year later, he ran a half-marathon and a triathlon. He lost 60 pounds and had become a runner. There wasn't anything complicated about his process. He believed he could do it, he believed he should do it, and he did it.

We will follow the same process with virtue. In this chapter, we'll think about ways to change ourselves into the virtuous people we know we can be. First we'll talk about what kind of character we're looking for, then we'll commit to becoming that person. Then we'll do it.

Getting Started

To change ourselves, we need an ignition point of some kind. Sometimes this comes in the form of a warning that our health is in danger. Sometimes we discover we will become parents and decide we need to change our ways to provide a good environment for someone else. Sometimes, we just wake up one day and realize we want to change. Some of these influences come from outside ourselves, but we must choose the change for ourselves if it is to be genuine. Some things in life we can choose, and some things we can't. The kind of stuff we're talking about here is the kind we can choose. We can choose to change ourselves into virtuous people. If you've gotten this far, you've probably made that choice. Now you want some ideas on how to go about it.

The hardest part is over. You've made the decision. When you believe an idea, deep down, your body believes it, too. It's not just mental. Your physical actions are a result of your mind's choices. If you think of yourself as strong and confident, your posture will reflect that. If you think of yourself as gentle and open to contact with other people, your arms will seldom be crossed over your chest. Our bodies reflect our intellectual choices in ways we often do not even notice.

People who believe it is important to drink half a gallon of water every day always have water nearby. They drink it without thinking about it. It is just what they do.

People who don't approve of littering pick up trash when they see it. It is not a big sacrifice. They aren't thinking that someone else will get it, because they understand that all of us are the "someone elses."

You can think of other examples of physical activities that follow naturally from belief. Physical habits and practices come from our internal beliefs.

Now let's see what we can do about putting some specific virtues into practice.

Courage

Courage is choosing to do things even though we are afraid. You have decided to be a person of courage. You want it to come naturally and to grow out of who you are. You don't want it to be a special quality you summon when danger appears; you want your courage to be a daily series of actions and choices. At some point, courage becomes a quality that is not so much a response to a fear but an overall approach to life and its challenges.

Let's think of some ways to put courage into action. The idea is to live within that golden mean, not to be reckless or foolhardy, and not to be a coward. We want to think of activities that you may have avoided because you were afraid of them, and to choose one that is worth the risks. What are the risks? Most of us have fears of failure and fears of success.

A fear of failure will keep you from trying something because you are afraid of doing it very badly, or even a little badly. You are afraid that others will see, and will laugh at you or not respect you. These are not always good enough reasons to shy away from an attempt. I suppose if you want to be an eye surgeon and it turns out you do not have the requisite talent and cannot learn it, you probably should not proceed with this activity because you could harm others. If you want to be a defensive end for a football team, though, and you do not have the requisite talent, there is little harm in your trying to learn it. As long as you learn how to tackle properly, you are unlikely to harm anyone but yourself in the attempt. You may even accomplish your goal. You will never know until you try.

A fear of success is even more insidious for me. This means I avoided some activities because I knew there was a good chance I would be good at them, and that people would come to expect me to always be good at them. This kind of pressure is more self-driven than the fear of failure, although both have a lot to do with what other people think of us. A fear of success kept me from trying teaching, but the first day I tried it on my own, I discovered that it fit me nicely.

I can recommend two ways to overcome these kinds of performance-based fears. The first is to imagine the worst-case scenario. If you fail at something, what is the worst that can happen? If it's just that you feel silly or foolish, that's really not so bad. If you try to paint a picture and it turns out horribly, so what? No one has been harmed. Perhaps you might have used the time you spent on the painting for something more "worthwhile," but you also might have learned something about yourself in the process.

We learn all kinds of things about ourselves from failing at sports. Some sports emphasize how often we fail and that success is rare indeed. When we lose games, we learn how to behave toward the winning opponent. We learn how to tell ourselves that our value as a person is not weighed by our success at a sport. We learn to pay attention to these more important lessons, so that the end of the day and the end of a life matter far more than the details of how we got there.

So the first step is realizing that failure (or success, if that is your fear) is not the end of the world in most cases. You are smart enough to sort out activities in which you can harm others, or significantly harm yourself, and to consider those activities with even more care. The second step toward conquering fears is to do the things that spark them.

People who are afraid to speak in public eventually get past it by doing it. They start small, repeat it several times, and gradually increase the size of the group until they are no longer paralyzed by being in front of an audience. Those first several attempts can be terrifying. This is where we are showing courage, by continuing to try something that scares us. If the first few attempts are successful, the speaker has good energy on which to build. If the first few attempts are failures, in a way it becomes harder to continue because it seems you may not get better. The good news is that nearly always, some aspect of the experience goes well: a joke reaches the audience, or you can see that a listener has understood a key point. Keeping on the path toward getting better requires fortitude at this juncture. This is where we draw on our courage and the courage of the person we want to become.

The second step toward overcoming fears is to act on them. We become courageous by acting in courageous ways. At first we have to choose to act with courage, because it does not always come naturally. Doing this requires an act of will. After having made that choice over and over for a while, it becomes more natural. I also find that considering a problem before it happens, and choosing a solution, makes it much easier to handle the situation when it arises. This way, you do not have to rely on yourself to make the hard choices in the heat of a moment. You have already chosen, and now you only have to act. This pre-planning can be part of the process of becoming a courageous person.

You might imagine what you would do if a particular catastrophe befell you and think about actions you would take to make the situation better. My dad used to give us quizzes about driving -- such as if he was driving and he was to have an epileptic seizure and I was in the front seat next to him, what was the first thing I should do? First is to grab the steering wheel. Next is to find a way to stop the car. Back then you could just turn off the ignition key, but on modern cars, turning off the key locks the steering wheel. So don't do that. I guess the passenger can put the car into neutral on most vehicles, hit the flashers, and coast to a stop. Then you can deal with the incapacitated driver. You have figured out that the first priority is to remove the car from the road, as it is a weapon that can get you and others hurt. Because you have that in mind now, if you're ever in a car when something goes wrong, you'll remember the drill and not panic.

I'll suggest a third fear that holds us back sometimes: the fear of the unknown. Human beings have imagination that can foresee a future with good and bad things in it. Far fewer of us see futures with good things. Doing so is a deliberate choice not everyone has learned how to make. Fear of the unknown is also augmented by fear of failure; we are afraid that we'll try something new and flop at it, so we decide we're better off staying where we are rather than risking the flop. People stay in jobs they hate for this reason. People who embrace change are the ones who can see a positive result from their risk. They are not so weighed down by the past that they fear either success or failure but are content to take what comes and make the best of it. You may need to choose this strategy through an act of will. You may have to confront your approach thus far and acknowledge that you have too often been guided by fears. If you can see the benefits of a life without those fears, now is the time for you to use an act of will to say, "I will not be ruled by fear any more."

In Aldous Huxley's *Brave New World*, most of the citizenry prefers sameness and predictability. They don't want excitement or very much stimulation. Inertia is both the tendency of a thing in motion to stay in motion and of a thing at rest to stay at rest. This "at-rest-ness" is very powerful once you get to a place where you are not really unhappy. It takes two things to break out of it: a desire for more, and (you guessed it) courage. In Huxley's society, most of the people simply have no desire for more; it's been bred out of them. We do not have that handicap. We know we are capable of goodness, and we aspire to it.

One of my favorite movies is *The Shawshank Redemption*. It is about hope. It crystallizes what hope is. Hope is not only an abstract thing that goes on inside your head or your heart. It is the actions you take every day toward making that hope real. One of the main characters puts it all into place when he says, "Get busy livin', or get busy dyin'." He means that if you are resigned to a life of defeat and failure, that's probably what you'll get. If you choose hope, you must put it into action. You cannot wait for someone else to come along and save you. You must save yourself.

I am not saying you can't participate in a religious system that includes help from outside yourself. We'll get into this more in the final chapter. What I'm saying is that your faith must be enacted by you. If you are not committed to acting out your hope and your belief in yourself, it will not matter if someone tries to redeem you. You cannot become a virtuous person if you do not act in virtuous ways yourself. You may draw strength from elsewhere if you need to, but you must be the virtuous person yourself. Courage, in this instance, is about you realizing that you are the one who must get out in life and live. You are not going to stand on the sidelines and wait for someone else to tell you when to play. You are going to get out there and run.

Generosity

Generosity is putting other people ahead of yourself. The golden mean for generosity is a place where you think of others most of the time, but you still allow time for yourself. If you do not take care of yourself, no one else will do it for you. Once you have done that, though, there is plenty of your energy that will be well-directed at other people. They need whatever you have to give, whether it is your talent or your time. Your willingness to help them is the biggest part of your gift.

The first step toward becoming a generous person is paying attention to what other people need and want. Too many of us are too wrapped up in our own needs and wants that we cannot or will not see those of others. The willingness to listen to others and to see what they may not see for themselves is a rare talent but one that you will learn to develop. It gets better with practice, like most things. One friend of mine did this so well, he noticed something I wanted, and then waited nearly a year to track it down and send it to me. By then I had forgotten my initial excitement, but his explanation brought back all of my original feelings. I was not only happy to have the gift but was thrilled he had (1) noticed I wanted it, and (2) followed through on that wish. I would never have bought it for myself, which made it even better. His noticing what someone else wanted is too rare, although I should say it is not that rare in my circle of friends. We do not stay close to each other if we don't have that quality. It is a requirement.

The first step is an awareness of other people; the second step is deciding whether you can make their needs happen. Not everybody should have everything she wants, and not all of us are equipped to satisfy all of those needs. We must be realistic and help the people we know how to help. We cannot save every starving child in Africa, but maybe we can help the lady next door by taking her newspaper to the front porch from the curb. Our sphere of influence is limited, although each of these small gestures has a ripple effect. Eventually we will live in a world where the little things have added up to a world without hunger. It is up to us to tackle these little things.

I should mention that it is possible to be excessive in your generosity. There are two ways to do this. One is to give money or time, and to want the appreciation of others for having done so. The very nature of generosity means that you do not need the recognition of others for it to have been worthwhile and good. Avoid the trap of giving only when others can see.

The second way to be excessive about generosity is when you give too much. This is a hard thing to quantify, because most of us could stand to give more of ourselves to others and may not approach a point where we have gone too far. If you run community meetings, volunteer time at local organizations, and do any number of other generous activities, you could reach a point where you try to do too much. Sometimes we try to do too much, and we do none of it well. It is better to contribute where we can and save some small time for ourselves than to give all of our energy to others and to save none for ourselves. A good way to tell if you have gone too far is to notice how often you are sick. If you rarely get sick, you probably have a good balance of energy toward the world and toward yourself. If you are often sick, you may need to spend a little more energy on yourself and a little less on others. You cannot help others if you are not healthy yourself.

It is not easy for me to think of examples of ways to be generous. At this point, it is not something I plan to do; it just happens. You want to pay attention to those around you, to listen to them with care. Sometimes they will say what they wish they had or wish someone would do for them. Sometimes -- and this is the part where being generous is really fun -- they do not say specifically what they need or want. You have to figure it out - and you have to figure out if just listening is all it takes. Solving a mystery is creative, challenging work. You will be very proud of yourself the first time you try it, and it works.

I will provide one suggestion for starting down the path toward generosity. Buy some nice postcards or stationery. Write a note to a friend or family member. It can be about nothing special, just a "thinking of you" message. Think with care about that person and something fun or special you did together. Write about that. Say you remember how good it felt when you climbed that mountain together or shared that cup of espresso together. If you have not been able to share a moment with your friend in a while, make the note be about your wish to spend time together. This activity will ask you to put some energy into your relationship with someone else. It will please the other person to know you were thinking of her. It will remind your friend why you like him. It will remind you to think about other people and to be grateful for the connections you have with other people.

It could be that generosity comes from being grateful for what we have and wanting to share with others. Any action that comes from gratitude is bound to make the world warmer.

Authenticity

"Should you fail to pilot your own ship, don't be surprised at what inappropriate port you find yourself docked." -- Tom Robbins, *Jitterbug Perfume*

We will not blame our mistakes on our pasts. We will not avoid the hard choices we must make. We will not try to run away from our true natures, and why should we? We are trying to make our true natures those of goodness. We will begin our path by acknowledging the kinds of people we have been in the past. We will not deceive ourselves about who we are. We will be totally, brutally honest with ourselves. Only then can we be honest with others.

If you have been framing yourself in a particular way that is not genuine, stop right now. Once you make up your mind to do it, you have done it. There is no room for any more self-deception. Examine yourself, all of your good traits and all of your flaws. Be honest about them. Root out all of the secrets you have been keeping from yourself. Uncover the hidden fears. You can pay a therapist to help if you like, but for the work to be authentic and useful, you must do it all yourself. The purpose of a good therapist is to help you stay away from known dead-ends. If you are watchful, you can do that yourself.

The road to authenticity is not necessarily smooth. You have a lot of old habits to unlearn. If you have been telling yourself that you are unworthy of love or the esteem of others, I'll bet your posture reflects that. I'll bet your shoulders are drawn in and your back is hunched. I tell you now, if you can convince your body that you are worthwhile, eventually your mind will also believe it. Notice your posture and correct it several times a day. This is not about making yourself look a particular way for the benefit of others. This is about making yourself genuine and healthy.

There are so many kinds of self-deception. You must identify the ones you have been using and simply stop them. They are harmful, some more than others. I guess the most common forms of self-deception are those in which we tell ourselves something about our performance. We tell ourselves we are very good at our jobs, or at singing in church, or at playing softball. These are not always true. We want to believe we are good at these things, so we tell ourselves we are. The other common deception is that we tell ourselves we are very bad at something. If we think we're bad at something, we have a built-in excuse to avoid it.

All of this rooting out of bad feelings requires courage, so you are building two virtues at once. It feels bad to uncover some of this negative energy, but you feel much better once it is out in the open. Acknowledging our faults is the first step toward owning them and toward banishing them. Once you believe you must stop a behavior, you are on the road toward stopping it. Each day as you notice yourself acting on deception, you can change that behavior. One step at a time.

In everyday life, how do we go about being authentic? You are a member of groups, but you do not have to conform to everything those groups do and believe. You do not have to choose your clothing or haircut based on what a group thinks looks good. You are free to decide those things for yourself. You may find that some of the group no longer wants to spend time with you because of your new haircut. Possibly those people were less interested in you than they were in the way you looked. You are better off without them. You want to spend time with people who appreciate the you who is inside you. It is far more important to know who you are and stand still inside that person, than that you run, run, run, to keep up with a crowd whose values you do not share so that you can feel the comfort of a group. It is not worth giving up yourself.

Aristotle talked about "accidental characteristics," things about us that could be otherwise, such as our skin color, height, or our place in society. These are things over which we have little or no control. He believed that what was more important about human beings was their essence. It is more important that you focus on the things that make you YOU than on things that are irrelevant. It should not matter what clothes you wear or the color of your eyes. Your worth as a person has nothing to do with those outer, superficial characteristics. They could be otherwise. What matters is the essence, the person who strives for a virtuous state of soul. It almost does not matter if we achieve this state of soul, only that we try and that we do so with all of our hearts.

Pride

The golden mean of pride, as we said in Chapter 2, is the middle ground between the excesses of egotism and vanity, and pride's deficiency, the lack of self-esteem. Each of these situations has its own path toward the middle.

If you lack self-esteem, be sure to read the previous section on authenticity to begin your transformation. You need to be able to take pride in your work at being good, or you will not continue it. There is little point in working toward goodness if you are not patting yourself on the back just a little bit, and reminding yourself that you are striving toward goodness for the best reason. Goodness is its own reward. The daily work we do on it is all the reward we need.

We defined egotism earlier as an improper appreciation of your own goodness. This is inappropriate either because you are not so good as you believe, or because you have more energy attached to being good than you should. Using the brutal self-examination of the previous section on authenticity will help you figure out which one is the case. If you are not as good as you think, work toward becoming more virtuous. Hint: Start with generosity. It is rarely a bad idea to think of other people before yourself. If your self-examination results in you seeing that you have been congratulating yourself too often on your virtuousness, you have an easy fix. Stop it. When you catch yourself paying attention to your own goodness, find somewhere else to put that energy. Hint: Start with thinking of someone else. It is rarely a bad idea to think of other people before yourself.

The last excess of pride is vanity, which we earlier described as the pattern in which you need the approval of others in order to appreciate your goodness. I suggest that usually this results from low self-esteem, because if you believed yourself good, you would not need others to say so. Therefore, choose to believe in your own goodness, and stop seeking the approval of others. As you grow in authenticity and courage, you will find you do not need that approval.

Another way to think about change

English writer Iris Murdoch had an interesting way to think about our goodness. As I understand her, she proposes we focus on ongoing morality, rather than on individual moments of choice. This is to say, much like Plato and Aristotle, that if we cultivate a character that is intent on goodness, when goodness comes along we will be naturally drawn to do it, appreciate it, embrace it.

She says she borrows Simone Weil's word "attend," which for me has connotations of constant consideration and a willingness to engage in details. It is in the details that we shape our characters. The big decisions become not so big after we spend a life making the little things right. In "The Idea of Perfection," she specifies that this attention is a characteristic of an "active moral agent," (33) a person who is active not only in moments of choice but at all times. "When I deliberate the die is already cast. Forces within me which are dark to me have already made the decision." (35)

This idea reminds me of French thinker Henri Bergson, who compared our life experience to that of a snowball rolling downhill, picking up a new layer with each turn. We cannot help but be the person we are because of our experiences, and we cannot help but consider possibilities as we go, opening ourselves to new ones so when a fork appears in the road, we naturally choose one path or the other. Says Murdoch, "The moral life . . . is something that goes on continually." (36)

Her title comes from her notion that we are "infinitely perfectible," as Plato thought. Both understood we will never "arrive" at wherever perfection "is," but that our nature is to make the attempt.

Murdoch is also a little reminiscent of William James, in that she understands that our action-taking in the world makes a difference both to ourselves and to the world. "Overt action can release psychic energies which can be released in no other way." (42) The physiological manifestation of our intention to be moral makes us moral in ways we cannot articulate. Our bodies become accustomed to performing moral acts; like a baseball player who habituates himself to swinging a bat, we create "muscle memory" in ourselves of what it feels like to do the right thing. We habituate ourselves to goodness.

John Stuart Mill said that the will is responsive to habit; we can train ourselves to let our conscience guide, rather than our desires. This comes first from making virtue seem a worthwhile goal and associating it with pleasure.

The Chicago Cubs nearly made it to the World Series in 2003. I had been a fan for ten years, joining a tradition of fans who supported the lovable losers. Perennial underdogs, the Cubs finally had all the pieces that year. They lost in the first round of the playoffs, though, and I had to say I was relieved. The much-anticipated matchup between the Cubs and Boston Red Sox didn't happen. The Cubs last won the World Series in 1908, the Red Sox in 1912. No teams had been without a title for so long.

Why was I relieved my team didn't reach the ultimate series? I would not have known what to do if they had won.

I had become so accustomed to rooting for a team that seldom played well enough to win anything meaningful, I would not have known what to do if they had pulled it off. It would have transformed all of us who were fans of losers to being fans of winners. It would have changed us. It would have become a product, and I had so enjoyed the process that I would have been disappointed. It is like the process of transforming ourselves into virtuous people.

You knew I would bring us back to virtue somehow. I don't intend to compare supporting a losing team to the pursuit of a virtuous life, except in the sense that each requires a long-term commitment and a daily effort. Like being a Cubs fan, the pursuit of virtue has no recognizable reward in sight except that it is worthy as an end in itself. By striving for virtue, we become virtuous. It is that simple.

CHAPTER 6

Imagine There's No Heaven

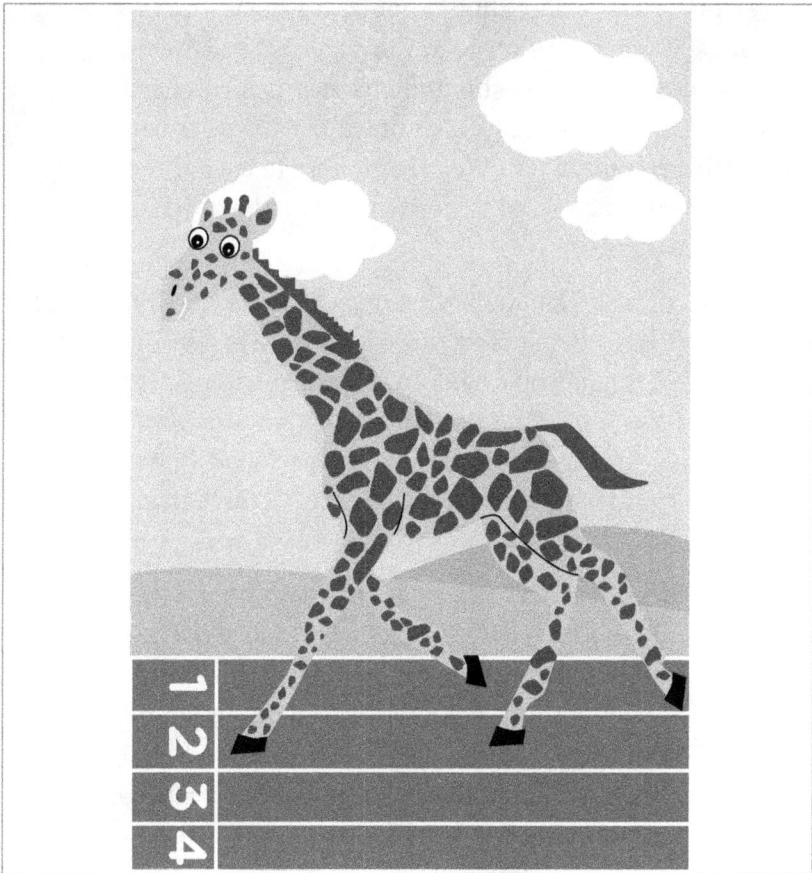

John Lennon had an insight in 1971's "Imagine" -- a song that gets my vote for the most important lyric ever written. He wanted us to ask us to think about ourselves and our actions without appealing to a god for meaning. I am especially intrigued by questions of why we should be moral beings regardless of a deity. Many religious systems rely on the threat of such a being to keep people in line. A reward in the next life, or even our current one, should not be the basis for our choosing to treat each other with respect. I'm eager to see a world in which we understand we should behave ethically regardless of how it affects us personally. Genuine altruism is rare enough that it must be cultivated. We are not here to earn things or to justify our existence. We are here to learn to be good, regardless of the consequences.

We have talked a lot about virtue in this book and about what virtue is. We have not spelled out what virtue is not. Virtue is not a list of rules, things you do because someone else says so. It is not a series of temptations you must resist in order to think yourself good. It is not an attempt to be perfect. None of us is perfect. To grasp what virtue is, maybe it will help if we can shed our old ideas and tell ourselves what virtue is not.

I walk around a track with my mom about once a week. We count laps. Once, after several laps, Mom said she felt virtuous. I asked what specifically she meant by that, and she said she felt good for doing something she knew was good for her but that she didn't want to do. I said I wished virtue could become things we do that are not difficult, that grow out of the people we have become. She asked whether I would rather be doing something else besides laps around a track, and I said not really. I know that exercise is a part of the person I am and of the person I want to become. It isn't an obstacle anymore; it's just what I do. That is what I mean about virtue not being a chore. After a while it is just what we do because we believe in it.

It's hardly on the same level, but one of my favorite quotes is by French thinker Henri Bergson, talking about saints. He says of people like Gandhi and Mother Teresa, "We cannot even say of this moral conviction that it moves mountains, for it sees no mountains to move." (*The Two Sources of Morality and Religion*, 1932, p. 53) I love that! For some folks, tackling a difficult chore is not even a chore, because it is just what needs to be done next. They know that someone has to do it, and in some instances, they are the best people to do it. So they put their heads down and do it. It is not a matter for whining and complaining, or for wishing for pats on the back afterward. It is just what they do. It is impossible to know The Good, and not to do the good. Plato said that somewhere.

When we see a task to accomplish that is a part of the person we are or want to be, it is not so difficult to get started doing it. What is difficult is when we see a task ahead that is not yet a natural outgrowth of the person we are. If you believe an activity or a habit is good for you, you will put it into practice and it will not be hard to do so. Your actions will grow out of the person you are. If you don't yet genuinely believe, you will not be able to do whatever it is. Some people have lots of trouble quitting smoking, as they are not completely convinced it is the person they wish to become. Some of us, though, realize that the person we want to become is not a smoker. So we quit. Immediately. It is not a struggle. The cessation of a bad habit grows naturally from the person and the person's state of soul. I'm not saying that smokers have bad states of soul. I'm saying that the kind of person who wants not to be a smoker, once she is totally convinced of that, one day is not a smoker. It can be that simple.

Sources of Morality

Aristotle believed that we somehow teach ourselves how to be excellent by using habit. Plato said that it is impossible to know the good and not to do the good. I want to suggest one other way of thinking about morality. Bergson's *The Two Sources of Morality and Religion* (1932), explains that the mass of humanity takes on moral behavior as a result of prohibition, a being told what to do by an outside source. These sources can be family, social groups, or religious traditions. He proposes that a rare few individuals do not see morality as a repressing of our desires to be selfish and bad. Rather, these rare few reach upward. They are motivated by aspiration rather than prohibition. These Mother Teresas and Ghandis are able to live without external moral codes; they create their own. They are the ones who advance our understanding of morality. They are not bound by rules and restrictions but are instead motivated by love of humanity.

I want to suggest that too often we are willing to blindly accept the rules given to us by our family or our community. Many of these rules end up being ones we adopt, but for them to be genuine, we must examine them and challenge them. If we become people of faith, at some point we must make a leap of faith. Following rules does not make us virtuous. We become virtuous when we study the nature of virtue and adopt it by choice rather than by rote.

I want us to observe speed limits because it is the right thing to do, not because we are afraid of getting a ticket. Fear of getting a ticket is not virtue. It is behavior modification. You can teach your puppy tricks the same way, but it is the tricks he learns on his own that will have more joy in them.

I want us to be kind to people we meet on the street -- not out of a sense of duty, but because we understand that friendliness and generosity are virtues.

I want us to be courageous and to admire courageous people, because standing strong in the face of fear is the fiercest challenge we have.

I want us to be genuine, authentic individuals, because it is our true nature to be honest with ourselves and with others.

I want us to notice our efforts and to take the right amount of pride in them, because we deserve respect.

I want us to see that virtue is its own reward. Virtue needs no reward. Virtue is an end unto itself.

Be good.

CHAPTER 7

We have opportunities to help others

World hunger is complicated. The late comedian Sam Kinison used to scream at the hungry in Africa that they should move out of the desert, because after all they could not eat sand. His act expressed the frustration we feel at a problem that is so large we feel we have no hope of solving it. I used to share some sympathy with the position that the world is overcrowded. I thought that maybe starvation is one way of keeping that overpopulation in check. I thought we might run out of room if some folks didn't go hungry sometimes.

I have changed my mind. Now I think if we choose our goals with care, we can eliminate world hunger. First, we must acknowledge we have an obligation to help those who will starve without us, if those folks got in that predicament through no fault of their own. I am not advocating permanent aid for someone who will not do her share to earn it, if she is able. Once we have identified worthy recipients, we help them. It is that simple.

1.5 billion people subsist on less than the equivalent of a dollar a day. Three billion people get by on less than two dollars a day. Many manage only subsistence. They have no hope of finding out their potential as human beings. It is all they can do to live from one day to the next. Thousands die every day. We have all seen the pictures. The United Nations World Food Programme says that 25,000 people die every day from hunger and poverty. Every day.

The everyday hunger of millions is overlooked -- maybe because it is not on the front page of the newspaper so often -- but the response to the December 2004 tsunami in Asia was tremendous. Governments and private citizens provided so much aid money in response that the American Red Cross said it had met its relief goal for that project for the next ten years. Contributions made after that announcement were diverted to other efforts in the International Response Fund. People gave too much. It is typical of the way we react to emergencies. We are good at rescue from dire emergency, but we refuse to understand that the folks going hungry all over the world are also in dire emergency. In the hour it took to start this chapter, 1,000 people died from preventable hunger and disease. They died from malaria, influenza and easily treatable diseases. People died who might have had access to treatment if they had been born north of the equator. Where you are born should not determine whether you live. We are all in this together.

One objection to providing money for aid agencies is that too much of the donations end up not going to feed the hungry, but to fund the bureaucracy needed to manage the agencies. I suggest that we have options other than this sort of inefficient agency. I suggest that we give actual food to local agencies, and that if we give money, we give it to the United Nations World Food Programme. We can choose toward what nation we wish our money to be directed, or we can indicate that it is to be used to help with any of several specific projects. I will revisit the option of giving to local agencies later.

The problem is solvable. It is not that there is not enough food. We would be in big trouble if we had to allocate scarce resources. but we don't. There is plenty of food. There are places where food goes to rot because there are no buyers. All we need is for an engineer or supply sergeant to figure out how to get it from place A to place B. The World Food Programme and like organizations perform this function with varying degrees of efficiency. The WFP responded very well to the tsunami emergency; it is equipped with mobile computers and has access to a satellite system to keep up with the food shipments.

Now that we understand the problem a little better, here is why we should help. One argument from a historical perspective is that colonization harmed many areas in ways that are felt today. Powerful nations stripped poor ones of their resources, so the poor places had nothing to trade for food. This model is especially true in Africa but also in parts of Asia and South America. This argument relies on people to accept responsibility for acts of their ancestors. It works only until we decide we should not have to be responsible for what our great-great-grandparents did.

A second argument for helping those in poverty is that if we do not, they may feel they have a right to take our surplus. This argument is one some people use to discuss immigration limits so that the United States, in particular, is not overrun by the poor from other nations. As it is an argument based on responding to a threat, I am not satisfied with it. I want a positive reason to help, not a negative reason to prevent my stuff being taken.

I want an argument that does not appeal to guilt and that does not appeal to fear. I want an argument that explains why helping someone is the right thing to do, in and of itself. In "An Essay on Man," Alexander Pope said that virtue is its own reward. We ought not need anything else. Based on that premise, here is the argument why we should help the hungry: I ought to help someone in need because the other person's continued poverty diminishes us both.

It is that simple. I should help because I can. I should not help a person out of pity for him, because pity changes my motivation. It makes my action self-interested. Pity inspires me to help someone because I know I will feel good afterward. It is better to help someone out of pity than not to help at all, but it is even better to help someone out of a recognition that he is a human being just like I am. I help the other, not out of pity but out of respect. Jean-Paul Sartre's "Existentialism is a Humanism" shares this same idea: In order to will myself free, I must will the other free. If I believe I am worthy of freedom and respect, I must believe that other human beings are worthy of them also.

At some point I may reach a position where I cannot help others anymore without diminishing myself, and then I will have a choice to make. In *The Moral Demands of Affluence*, Garrett Cullity tells us about an "altruistically-oriented life" -- a life in which one chooses to give to others until there is just enough energy and money left to keep the giver going. Few of us are prepared to go to this extreme. Few of us are willing to give so much of ourselves. Those who do give most of themselves, though, radiate a serenity we non-givers cannot know.

I imagine that a life spent in service to others has a quality about it that renders meaningless our efforts to accumulate material goods and pile up accomplishments. I have experienced some small sense of that quality of service to others and am looking forward to gradually increasing my commitment. I understand the feeling of doing a right thing not because it seems hard, but because it seems easy. Part of what makes doing good easy is doing it over and over. We become habituated to it. We know what good is. Plato tells us it is impossible to know The Good and not to do The Good. Bergson saw the same thing.

As for world hunger, here is my solution: I will do one thing at a time. I will start with one blood donation, one $10 gift to UNICEF or the Red Cross or the WFP or an organization I trust. It will be a while before I have to decide whether my giving is cutting into my own capacity to thrive. Until then, I will know I am increasing someone else's capacity to thrive. This kind of service to others is not painful. When it becomes painful, maybe all it will mean is that I am beginning to make a difference. We all have a great capacity for service, a capacity that too often goes untapped.

Why we must aid others

It is not enough that we refrain from harm. We must enable others to thrive, when it is in our power to do so. Cullity argues that the affluent should help the poor. He starts with Peter Singer's Life-Saving Analogy, which describes a child drowning in a pond in front of us. Singer says we must help a dying person right in front of us if it is at little expense to ourselves, and if we will not be compromising anything of comparable moral importance. Cullity wants to use this analogy to examine why we feel differently about helping people who are not directly in front of us. He explains that it is simply human nature, human psychology, to respond to a dire emergency nearby, whereas we are not as affected by distant emergencies. It is not that we are monsters; we are just wired this way. I think he is correct, that we are more inclined to help those nearby than those far away. An emergency in front of us has an immediacy that we cannot ignore.

If this is true that we want mostly only to help those nearby, it need not keep us from helping the hungry. There are plenty of hungry people in the United States, in our own cities. We can find ways to help them, and know that we are making a dent in the problem. We can do this first, and then we can think about how to think of the world as our neighbors. We will figure out a way to understand that there is no Us and Them, but only all Us.

In 1985, a group of pop singers got together and recorded a song to raise money for world hunger efforts. The group called itself U.S.A. For Africa; the song was called "We Are The World." The lyric, by Lionel Richie and Michael Jackson, includes a line saying that we have to stand together as if we were one being. The lyricists understood that when we separate ourselves into groups, we make it harder to help each other. When we see the group as everyone on the globe, we have a chance to distribute the resources equitably.

The song also says it only takes you and me to fix things. This approach makes the solution graspable, because the writers have appealed to the idea that even a few individual people can make a difference. If enough you's and me's are willing, even a large problem can be solved. All we have to do is do what we know how to do. If everyone goes that far, we can accomplish great things.

How we will aid others

As I read it, Henry Shue's "Solidarity Among Strangers and the Right to Food" says that rights are granted by people to other people. I am relieved to see this perspective, as too often we hear that rights are granted by God or are natural. If one does not believe in God this assertion cannot hold. Also, God is not here to make sure the rights are actually awarded. People must do this, so it must be that the rights come from people in the first place. Rights of some people lead to duties for other people (and also the people with the rights). If I assert a right to vote, someone will have a duty to staff the polling place. If I say my neighbor has a right to clean water, I have a duty to pay taxes so that the water can be cleaned. Rights are not given; they are granted. Someone has to make them happen.

I will use the United Nations 1948 *Universal Declaration of Human Rights* as a source for identifying rights and will discuss a few of them I find interesting. Most of these rights are ideas we take for granted in the United States. We presume we should have these things, and often we forget that in many areas of the world, they are not available. In an urban area with proper facilities, it is easy to say we want access to clean drinking water. These facilities do not exist everywhere. The declaration says lots of things should be available but does not explain how they are to be made available. It is up to us, and our governments, to make these things happen.

"Article 3. Everyone has the right to life, liberty, and the security of person." We understand that some persons give up their right to liberty if they commit certain crimes, but on the whole, liberty is a valued quality. We are offended that not everyone is free. Liberty itself is a positive right; freedom from persecution is a negative right. The distinction, I think, has to do with the person claiming a right rather than having someone else give it.

Articles 4 and 5 (paraphrased). Slavery and torture are wrong. Freedom from slavery and torture is a negative right. It requires that others refrain from enslaving me or torturing me.

"Article 13. (1) Everyone has the right to freedom of movement and residence within the borders of each state. (2) Everyone has the right to leave any country, including his own, and to return to his country." These freedoms are primarily negative; they require that others do not prevent me from moving about as I wish.

"Article 26. Everyone has the right to education. Education shall be free, at least in the elementary and fundamental stages. Elementary education shall be compulsory." I believe this article to be unrealistic. Most of the the other articles describe conditions that do not require funding, only a commitment to fairness. This article requires money. Education is not free. It cannot be free. Someone must pay for it. In governmental systems in which education has a high priority, taxpayers fund the school systems. It is not free. Possibly it is free to some users, but only because it is a drain on others. This is the perfect example of a right that requires a duty. A child's right to education is paid for in part by her neighbor, who does not have children. This is not a burden because most of us understand that educating children is a good thing for us all. But it is not free.

Negative rights are those things we believe we should not have to be burdened with in order to live freely. We should not have to drink unclean water or breathe unclean air; we should not have our ability to move about freely be encroached; we should not be afraid of others who would harm us. Freedom from vulnerability is a negative right.

With a right granted to me comes a duty on you. If I am not to be persecuted because of my religion, your duty is to refrain from persecuting me. If I am not to have to drink impure water, your duty is to refrain from polluting the stream. These are negative duties. When we agree to them, we pledge not to harm each other.

Positive rights are similar in that they are rights, but they have another component that negative rights do not. Positive rights describe ways in which we expect to be able to fulfill our potential. Positive rights require that we have access to as many possibilities as we can, especially education. The ability to thrive is a positive right.

Positive rights also create duties. The distinction from negative rights is that a positive right creates duties in others but also in the person who is claiming the right. If you exercise a right to participate in government, I must provide the opportunity for you to do it, and you must vote. If you say you have a right to a free education, I must provide the school, and you must attend. Later, you must help provide the school for the next person. Positive duties require us to act, or there would be no need to have ethical systems. Positive rights and duties are what we call proactive. You cannot sit around and wait for someone else to free you. In *The Ethics of Ambiguity*, Simone de Beauvoir told us that "Freedom will never be given; it will always have to be won."

If we can grant that people in the world are entitled to certain privileges by virtue of their being here, we can acknowledge our own ability to make some of those privileges real. We can act. First, we can expend our energy to make life better for people we already know. Then we can notice our neighbors, and do what we can to help them reach their potential. From there it seems a simple step to aiding those people we will never know, those who live in other parts of the globe.

I once received an unanticipated chunk of money. In memory of a former colleague, I was able to donate some of it to a fellowship program that helps South African journalists. Two years later, I was asked to give a mini-tour of the production departments at *The Charlotte Observer* to a visiting journalist. He was an editor at a South African newspaper, learning about American methods. We had a nice chat, and later I found out he had been visiting on a grant paid for by the very program to which I had given money. This stuff really does come back to us, in ways that give us pleasant goose bumps.

Whatever goodness and joy we have experienced, we did not get here on our own. Others helped us. We need to get moving on returning that help. Doing so does not mean we are acting out of guilt but out of gratitude.

WORKS CITED

Bergson, Henri. *The Two Sources of Morality and Religion*, trans. R. Ashley Audra and Cloudesley Brereton. Notre Dame, Ind.: University of Notre Dame Press, 1977 (originally published 1932).

Cullity, Garrett. *The Moral Demands of Affluence*. Oxford: Clarendon Press, 2004.

de Beauvoir, Simone. *The Ethics of Ambiguity*. New York: Kensington Publishing Corp., 1976.

Shue, Henry. "Solidarity Among Strangers and the Right to Food." *World Hunger and Morality*, 2nd edition, ed. William Aiken and Hugh LaFollette. Upper Saddle River, N.J.: Prentice Hall, 1996.

United Nations Universal Declaration of Human Rights. Retrieved May 2005: www.un.org/Overview/rights.html

United Nations World Food Programme. Retrieved May 2005: www.wfp.org

Parts of Chapter 7 first appeared in *The Charlotte Observer* on June 12, 2005.

SAMPLE VIRTUES

compassion	courage	thoughtfulness
loyalty	generosity	friendliness
patience	self-discipline	authenticity
forgiveness	moderation	appropriate pride
fairness	integrity	appropriate anger

www.ingramcontent.com/pod-product-compliance
Lightning Source LLC
Chambersburg PA
CBHW020512030426
42337CB00011B/345